The Great Pyramid

and the Sphinx

Damien Pryor

The essential handbook to the monuments of Giza

Also available by this author:
The Great Pyramid and the Sphinx
The Externsteine: Europe's greatest Celtic site
Stonehenge: The essential guide to its purpose and context
The tropical zodiac, its origin and validity; the origin
of the zodiac signs

ISBN 9780958134149

Ancient Egypt: The Great Pyramid and the Sphinx
The Essential Handbook on the Monuments of Giza

CONTENTS

Initiatory room hidden in a temple at Karnak
A new attitude from younger Egyptologists
The pyramid of Khafre (Chephren)
Khafre's Valley Temple
A tomb and an initiatory temple
The underground Osiris Chamber

CHAPTER ONE   An overview of the Giza monuments

Introduction: the three purposes of the Giza monument
On the Giza plateau is located the most famous group of sacred monuments in the world. Just beyond the outskirts of Cairo, amidst a variety of other lesser temples and tombs, three pyramids and the enigmatic great sphinx tower majestically and enigmatically above the restless sands of the Saharan desert. The Sphinx and the Great Pyramid of Khufu arouse a ceaseless fascination worldwide.

The strange architectural designs inside the Great Pyramid contribute to the extraordinary fascination that this monument exerts. Inside the Great Pyramid is a series of enigmatic rooms and passageways, whose designs seem to point to a significance much greater than current explanations allow. And rumours of tunnels under the sand connecting the two monuments together, and of undiscovered chambers, add fuel to this fascination. So potent is the fascination which these monuments excite that they have long been the subject of a potent, and at times obsessive, interest.

But even without these supposed secret chambers and tunnels, the monuments on the Giza plateau are profoundly interesting and deeply thought provoking. As we shall see later in this book, to really enter into the core of what these monuments really mean, we need to know that there are three different Giza plateaus, so to speak. Then we can begin to appreciate the greatness of what the ancient Egyptians achieved, and the religious attitude and spiritual insights behind it.

There is firstly, the Giza plateau as the embodiment of the primordial moment when the Earth first emerged from the primordial vast cosmic ocean of spirit, called Nun, through the powers of the sun god Ra. Secondly, there is the plateau as a site with awe-inspiring buildings and monuments that were dedicated to religious-spiritual practices. This includes rituals for the priestly task of worshipping the great sun god Ra or

Osiris, and Ra-Harmakhis (the Sphinx), and for contemplating a central theme of Egyptian religious truths, the resurrection of Osiris. As we shall see, this activity included rites of an initiatory nature, which were held for example, at the secretive underground Chamber of Osiris situated on the causeway built for Khafre's pyramid.

And thirdly, the Giza Plateau became in the course of time a very large necropolis or burial site, with several thousand tombs. There are also several mortuary temples, designed for the rituals needed by the souls of the dead, especially by the pharaohs, on their journey in the after-life. The ancient Egyptian priesthoods had an extraordinarily detailed and profound view of the after-life, and many of these beliefs are portrayed on the walls of the tombs.

The three main pyramids, that of Khufu (or in Greek, Cheops), Khafre (or Chephren) and Menkaure (or Mycerinos) became the hub around which many other monuments were constructed. Clustered near the two larger pyramids are tombs or mastabas of people from the upper classes of ancient Egypt, creating what is known as the mastaba fields. And in addition, eight small pyramids were constructed as tombs. There are also several temples, the two most significant are near the great Sphinx; they are the Valley Temple of Pharaoh Khafre, and the Old Kingdom Temple of the Sphinx. The remains of another, much later Temple of the Sphinx is still to be seen, off to the north of the sphinx, dedicated to the deity Horemakhet, built by Amenhotep II, in the New Kingdom (about 1400 BC).

There is a temple for Menkaure and for Khafre, (and the remains of one for Khufu) adjoining their pyramids, and there are also underground chambers; for example, pits in which a funeral-boat was placed, to be used by a Pharaoh as he ascends up to the stars, in his soul. In addition there are large causeways, the most prominent being a causeway leading from Khafre's pyramid down to the sphinx. Another feature here is the Wall of the Crow, or Heit el-Ghourab as it called in Arabic. It is a massive and ancient stonewall, 200 metres (656 feet) long, a few hundred yards to the south of the Sphinx. Some distance away from the main monuments, it was a considerable undertaking, as it is some 10 metres high (33 feet), and ten metres thick at the base, and was built in the Old Kingdom times.

Archaeologists currently believe that it was constructed to act as a kind of dyke, protecting the main monuments from flash flooding. This theme of flash flooding is important, and we shall encounter it again when studying the sphinx. But it also demarcates the general area of the religious monuments on the plateau from the area where pragmatic buildings were located, namely the workmen's camp, grain silos, workmen's cemetery, etc.

See illustration 1, which shows clearly the position and layout of all these various monuments on the Giza plateau. We shall undertake a journey into the heart of this amazing sacred site, by exploring the core meanings of the three types of monuments here, or the three different faces of the Giza Plateau. But first we will just briefly consider the most significant of all the fascinating features of the site, the Great Pyramid.

The Great Pyramid: the astonishing basic facts
The Great Pyramid is a really imposing monument, originally reaching up146.5m (481 feet), and covering some 13.5 acres (5.5 hectares). Despite the obvious damage done to its outer layers of stonework, it is still imposing even at close quarters, because of its vast size. One is almost overwhelmed by a feeling of being reduced to a tiny insignificant creature, when standing near this mountain of stone blocks, assembled with such technical perfection. How much more potent its impact would be, if the original polished limestone casing, had not been dislodged by a violent earthquake centuries ago!

1   THE GIZA PLATEAU: A GENERAL OVERVIEW OF THE SITE (in earlier times)

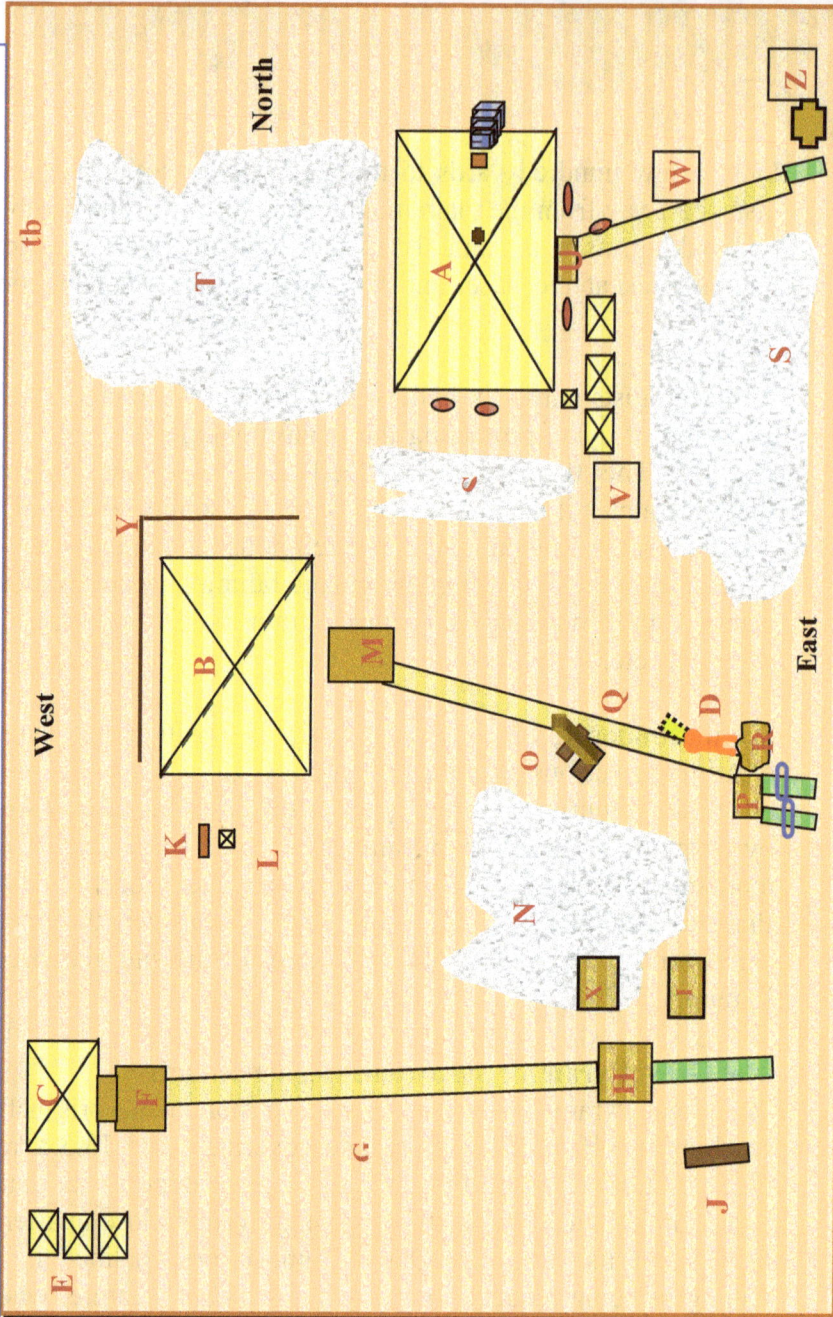

North

West

East

tb

A   Pyramid of Khufu / Cheops
B   Pyramid of Khafre (Chephren)
C   Pyramid of Menkaure (Mykineros)
D   Great Sphinx
E   Menkaure family pyramids
F   Menkaure ritual Temple
G   Menkaure Causeway
H   Menkaure's valley temple
I   Necropolis priests' houses
J   Wall of the Crow
K   Khafre serdab (ba tomb)
L   Khafre family pyramid
M   Khafre ritual temple
N   Central Mastaba (tombs) area
O   Underground Osiris chamber
P   Khafre Valley Temple
Q   Khafre Causeway
R   Sphinx Temple
S   Eastern Mastaba area
T   Western Mastaba area
U   Khufu ritual temple
V   Khufu family pyramids
W   Khufu Causeway (traces left)
X   tomb of Khentkawes
Y   Khafre quarry perimeter
Z   Khufu Valley Temple (destroyed)
tb = tomb of the birds

▬ Khufu solar boat pits
▬ Khafre solar boat pits
      ramps to water-ways (destroyed)
      dead-end tunnel from sphinx
      entry ramp Grt. Pyramid (assumed)
      Gash in upper wall of Pyramid
      hidden swivel-door entrance

4

Also the nearby pyramid of Pharaoh Khafre is nearly as huge; in fact it looks taller, being built on a higher rise of the plateau, and having a steeper angle to the walls. It still has some of its limestone casing left around the upper layers of stones. Entry into the Great Pyramid is only possible as the result of the actions of an Arabian ruler in the ninth century, who in his quest for fabulous treasure, had his workmen smash their way into the interior, only to find no riches of any kind.

Today, access is still gained via the opening made into the side of the great building by these workmen, but today electrical lighting, hand-rails and wooden planks make an exploration of its interior much less difficult than in the ninth century. The guidebooks say that the Great Pyramid was a tomb for the Pharaoh Khufu (called Cheops in Greek), who ruled about 4,600 years ago, in the 26th century BC (or perhaps a century or two earlier). Authorities aren't sure exactly when Khufu lived, the dates of his reign given by historians vary from 2551-2528 to 2789-2767 BC.

There is actually a lack of evidence with regard to the precise age of these monuments at Giza – a theme that we shall explore in some detail. Apart from a few hieroglyphs, found in a very inaccessible chamber high above the ceiling of the King's Chamber, there are very few direct indicators to link the Great Pyramid with Khufu. However the guidebooks may well be entirely correct, we shall find out about this later in the book.

But in fact little in the way of written texts about anything at all survives from such ancient times, for this was an age when wars and internal battles were occurring, in which many documents and monuments were destroyed. However, ancient Egyptian texts do describe Khufu (Cheops) as the Pharaoh responsible for its construction, and the other two pyramids as being constructed by his son Khafre (Chephren), and his grandson Menkaure (Mycerinos) respectively. Later we shall examine the question of the true age of the Great Pyramid very carefully, when we explore its various extraordinary features.

The Great Pyramid has spawned vehement disagreement between mainstream archaeologists and spiritually inclined people. Over-excited mystical researchers at times seek to carry out research that is damaging to the monument, and some have been banned from the Giza plateau. In earlier times, unprincipled tourists chipped away a sizeable part of the side of the sarcophagus inside the King's Chamber. The sarcophagus is a marvel of the rock carver's art, being made from a single slab of granite, apparently using only copper tools; an achievement hard to explain today. Before it was damaged by souvenir seekers, the sarcophagus was said to emit a melodious note, if lightly struck.

The purpose of the Great Pyramid has been a subject of dispute for centuries. Many nonsensical theories have been formulated to explain its existence. It is said by some, whose research is driven by Biblical fundamentalism, that the internal chambers of the Great Pyramid are a mathematical code enabling the discerning researcher to predict the return of Christ, and also the end of the world, etc. Others have declared, incorrectly, that the shafts in the chambers were aligned to four significant stars in the heavens at a certain year in the ancient past, which then allows the date of its construction to be determined.

Carefully grounded research, which is open to holistic ideas, reveals that such extreme ideas have no basis in fact. Its real secrets and features are far more significant and profound than these ideas. For example, an ancient papyrus document which is now being taken seriously by mainstream Egyptologists, reveals that its design and internal chambers are linked to knowledge about cosmic and spiritual matters, from the fabled sage Hermes or Thoth, deeply revered by the ancient Egyptians.

A fluke aerial photograph from 1929 revealed that the walls of the Great Pyramid actually have an indentation in them, which could have allowed the sunlight at dawn to reflect off both of these the double walls, and make a bright reflection of light as the sun rose, at various times of the year. The Great Pyramid is aligned very accurately north-south. The extreme accuracy of its orientation has aroused a great deal of interest and speculation. Many scientific experts still today find the accuracy of its siting is beyond scientific explanation. We shall consider these features and many others too, in this book.

The Great Pyramid is of enormous interest to many mystically inclined people in the Western world, who believe that its primary purpose was to facilitate the work of the priesthood in training its priests to experience the realms of spirit. These are the realms where it was believed that the great sun godRaor Osiris and many other deities dwell; and where the soul finds itself after death. This viewpoint is strongly rejected by the majority of Egyptologists, but not by all of them. The majority argue that there is not a single scrap of evidence to support the underlying idea here, namely that the ancient Egyptians developed a system of secret instruction and training in spiritual faculties.

But is there in fact a lot of evidence? We shall explore the evidence and logic behind both arguments, later on. The Great Pyramid is an integral part of an extensive burial site, a vast necropolis, and yet its internal architecture contains a symbolic element which hints at the process of becoming spiritually enlightened. To find out the answers to such questions, we need to set a path safely between the ungrounded theories, and short-sighted dogmas. So, what is the purpose of these world-famous monuments? As we mentioned earlier, there are really three, different but interrelated, purposes to these monuments.

The Giza Plateau One: as the place of the primordial Creation
Although the Great Pyramid has specific purposes of its own, we need to note firstly that this truly huge monument was of course built on a plateau, the Giza plateau, which gradually

rises some metres above the Nile River and its flood plain. This is significant to the design of the Great Pyramid, because it enables this site to represent key features in the Creation account of the ancient Egyptian religion. There are only a few accounts of the Creation story that have survived from ancient Egypt; so details have to be pasted together from references found in hymns, and funeral texts, etc. But in these sparse accounts, it is told how the Earth emerged out of a primordial ocean, through the power of a great deity called Ra, the sun god.

Interwoven within this activity or perhaps hidden within the actions of this sun god, was Atum, who has similar qualities to what the religions of the western world term, God. Now, the version of this story from the sacred town of Heliopolis is of special relevance, as later Egyptian texts indicate that the impetus to carve the great sphinx on the Giza plateau originally came from the venerated priesthood of Heliopolis, the supreme centre in Egypt for the cult of the sun god, Ra.

According to the creation story from the priesthood located at Heliopolis, as the Earth rose up from the primordial waters it appeared in the shape of a pyramidal mound. This mound became known as the Ben-Ben or Bennu. It is understood that the early Egyptian tombs, which were shaped like a truncated mound or mastaba were representations of this somewhat rounded pyramidal primeval Earth mound.

This act of creation so long ago, was a core theme in the mindset of the priests and people of the Old Kingdom. It was obviously as important to the Egyptians as the story of the Fall of Man is to the Judeo-Christian world. Each temple site of the ancient Egyptian people made especial effort to re-create this primordial creation, because it was so central to their relationship with the gods.

At Heliopolis a Ben-Ben stone was set up as the main sacred symbol of the sun god cult, and here this prominent sacred symbol became pyramidal in form, not just a rounded mound or a truncated slab. In the tradition taught at Heliopolis, on the primordial Day of Creation the Earth arose as a somewhat rounded pyramidal-shaped mass.[1] Eventually it became the custom for the top of a pyramid to be given a pyramidion, which is a hollow miniature pyramid to ensure its peak was true to the pyramidal shape. Such a miniature pyramid could also be placed on top of an obelisk. The word pyramidion in ancient Egyptian was ben-benet and this term is directly derived from ben-ben. One of the many funeral texts of ancient Egypt, written on the walls of tombs (no. 600), reads,

> "Atum-Kheprer (Atum within the sun-god) you have come to be high on the hill, you have arisen on the Ben-Ben stone in the sanctuary of….Heliopolis…"[2]

The different religious centres localized the actual place of creation, where the solid mound rose up out of the primordial, fluidic ocean (called Nun) to their own sacred site. So a myth from Hermopolis will say…"Ra who was on the hill which is in Hermopolis..." A myth from Thebes will speak of " the Island of Flames…the first primeval island out of the Great Flood". But we note that in the creation myths from Heliopolis, it is recounted how the sun-god appeared upon the pyramidal shaped ben-ben stone in the Temple of the Phoenix at Heliopolis. This confirms that the initiative to construct the monuments at Giza was closely linked to the influence of the priests of Heliopolis.

So, with the construction of the Great Pyramid, the Giza Plateau took on the appearance of the primordial Earth on the day of Creation. This was especially the case every summer when the Nile River flooded, and the plateau became partly surrounded by flood waters before the annual flooding of the

---

[1] R. H.Wilkinson, The Complete Gods and Goddesses of Ancient Egypt, Thames & Hudson, 2003; and see 'eternalegypt.org' website; E.A. Wallis-Budge, The Gods of the Egyptians 2 vols, Dover Pubs, N.Y. 1969; D. McKenzie, Egyptian Myths and Legends, Bell Publ. N.Y. 1978.
[2] www.Egyptologyonline.com/religion

Nile was obstructed by the construction of the Aswan High Dam, see illustration 2. Nearly all Egyptologists believe that the ancient Egyptians saw the Giza plateau with its pyramids as a reflection of the conical pyramidal Ben-Ben mound arising out of Nun. This Creation moment where the pyramidal Earth arose above the primordial waters was often included in the design of temples. An example of this can be seen with the mortuary temple of Mentuhotep.[3]

The Giza plateau was seen as mystically embodying in the present age, the time and place where the primordial Earth long ago arose out of the cosmic waters. This attitude of the ancient Egyptians is affirmed by some words on the famous Stele of Thothmes IV. This stele or inscribed upright stone slab, has an inscription on it which was written by pharaoh Thothmes IV, who reigned about 1,400 BC. Thothmes ordered the stele with its inscription to be placed between the paws of the sphinx. The text is about a spiritual experience that the pharaoh underwent whilst resting in the shade of the sphinx. He describes the Giza plateau as a place which is a necropolis, but which is also the place where the primordial creation of the Earth occurred.

That is, the Giza plateau is described as the place of Creation, where the Ben-Ben pyramidal mound arose. This idea was probably not just a theological allegory for the priests, but an existential spiritual truth. One gets the impression reading the old texts that the ancient priests had a similar experience to that of the Australian Aborigines, whose famous Dreamtime is a way of experiencing the environment spiritually, which merges together the past and the present. The stele inscription says in part,

> ....Then came Thothmes IV's time for allowing rest to his servants, at a locality consecrated to the gods,...... in the Necropolis {i.e., the Giza plateau}....which is...at that **sacred Place of the Creation**, the sacred path of

---

[3] See website http://www.freeegypt.info/Pages/274

the gods towards the western horizon of On (Heliopolis).

This phrase given here, in a translation from D. Mallet, " that sacred place of the Creation", in the hieroglyphics is literally "that sacred place of the first time". It can also be translated as "that sanctified place of the primeval time", as Christine El-Mahdy does in her German version, *(am geheiligten Platz der Urzeit).*[4] So when we visit Egypt and see the Giza plateau from a distance, especially from a boat on the Nile, we can pause to contemplate the sight of a plateau that rises up above the flood waters of the Nile, surmounted by the Great Pyramid, and see here a depiction of the creation of the Earth, when the pyramidal mound arose out of the primordial waters of the cosmos. Let's now consider the basic fact about the great Sphinx.

The great Sphinx: background information
Archaeologists generally date the sphinx to about 2,500 BC, that is to the reign of Pharaoh Khafre in the Old Kingdom of ancient Egypt. The sphinx is a striking sight; it is the world's largest monument carved from a rock outcrop, being some 74m (240 ft) long, 20m (66 ft) high. Its head is about9m long (30 ft) and 4.3m (14ft) wide at its widest part, and its famous paws are 15m (50 ft) long. Just beyond the sphinx are the remains of two temples. There is the Temple of the Sphinx, whose huge foundation stones are visible, but badly eroded. The stones used in building this temple were quarried from the area enclosing the sphinx. After they were removed, the Sphinx was shaped from the resulting hillock within its enclosing walls. Nearby is the Valley Temple of Khafre, with stonewalls in good repair.

The traveller gazes at these intriguing monuments, feeling that these ancient stone works mutely guard truths which were

---

[4] The stele of Thothmes IV; my English version formed from the English version of D. Mallet and the German version of Christine El-Mahdy, see (www.meritneith.de traumstele-thutmosis.htm) and incorporating comments from E.A. Wallis- Budge.

deeply valued in times long since gone. Some understanding of the mystical-religious meaning of the sphinx to ancient peoples helps one to appreciate the huge sphinx of Giza. We note in passing that the precision positioning of stone slabs, weighing up to 200 tons, appears to defy the capacity of modern engineering, let alone people from the Old Kingdom of Egypt. So we shall have a section devoted to this theme of unexplained engineering achievements.

We have noted above that the Giza plateau is in many respects a huge necropolis, but we also need to note that ancient cultures, including certainly the ancient Egyptians, were deeply involved in the veneration of spiritual beings, not only the deceased pharaohs (who were understood to be living among the stars). This means that the cult of the dead and the quest for becoming attuned to divine beings are actually closely intertwined themes in most ancient cultures.

For how can the priests offer a safe journey for the pharaoh into the Otherworld, if they have no claim to a knowledge of, or good-will from, the deities over there? A central deity in Egypt was the deeply revered sun god Ra (also known as Osiris) and another deity was Horus, who was the intermediary between the sun god and humanity. In addition there were other deities who were in effect aspects of the sun god. So what role did the great sphinx play in the spiritual-religious life of old Egypt, and why are these temples located so close to it?

As one gazes across to the huge and strangely elongated form of the sphinx from the tourist enclosure, one feels questions arising; when was it carved, and what does it mean? In fact, the question of how old any ancient site and its monuments may actually be, is very hard to answer. So as we explore the

2 THE GIZA PYRAMIDS AS THE DAY OF CREATION

Approximately how the Giza plateau with its pyramids would have looked, when the Nile River flooded.

For millennia each year in summertime the mountainous pyramids on the Giza plateau rose above the floodwaters of the Nile, like a pyramdion (a pyramidal apex). They thus became a symbol of the primordial Creation Day when the Earth, a pyramidal-shape (but rounded-out), emerged from Nun, the cosmic ocean, the matrix of all life.

age of the sphinx, we will get an idea of the controversial issues involved with any sacred site. Some earlier academic scholars, and some modern revisionists of Egyptian antiquity, put much weight on the fact that there is only slight evidence connecting the sphinx to pharaoh Khafre, the son of Khufu. They think that it might be a few decades older, or even a couple of centuries, because the generally accepted chronology of the Old Kingdom is often viewed as needing to be pushed back in time a little.

Thoughts as to whether the sphinx might not be a few centuries older than the accepted dating were voiced in the late 19th century by the very learned scholar E. A. Wallis-Budge. Other earlier Egyptologists, such as Gaston Maspero and Selim Hassan, also pointed out that the sphinx, whose sides are badly eroded, shows signs of having been exposed to extensive erosion, and may be a few centuries older than the time of Khafre.

But, by contrast to this modest, reasoned revision of the timescale, it is believed in mystical circles that the sphinx was not carved out of its rocky hill in ancient Egyptian times about 5,000 years ago, but rather, long ago in an ancient pre-diluvial world, some 11,000 years ago (or even 60,000 years ago). The American trance medium Edgar Cayce, and Madam Blavatsky, founder of the Theosophical Society, are prominent figures amongst Western mystical circles who date the sphinx to such remote ages.

Is this mystical view true, or is it all a huge mistake? And what is the sphinx anyway, why is it different from the classical sphinx of Mesopotamia and Greece ? And in recent years, writers such as John West, and a Boston geologist, Prof. R. Schoch, have made the astonishing claim that it may be about 10,000 years old. They develop their conclusions from geological ideas. They claim that such erosion as the sphinx exhibits is caused by falling rain, endured over millennia.

In effect this theory argues for a time of construction which occurred when Egypt and northern Africa were moist, fertile areas. It is believed in various circles that when the great Flood occurred, as recorded in the Bible and many other ancient texts, perhaps 9,000 years ago, there was severe climate impact, and this caused northern Africa to become a desert. But before then northern Africa was a fertile land. So the alternative theory could be called the pre-Flood or pre-diluvial theory of the origin of the Giza plateau monuments. This alternative theory would mean that the sphinx pre-dates the current desert climate of the Nile valley, thus putting its age at somewhere earlier than 7,000 BC, when the current dry climate began.

However, the argument advanced by Schoch, who thinks that not only the sphinx, but also the Great Pyramid, was constructed several millennia before Khufu, is now very much in doubt. Egyptologists and geologists have strongly and coherently argued against Schoch, saying that the erosion is indeed due to water as Schoch maintains, but it is not due to rain falling many millennia ago. It is from other causes; for example it is caused by moisture from dew condensing on the sphinx's outer layer, which dissolves the limestone. But above all, the erosion is caused by rain which lingers in the sand built up around the sphinx.

Over some 5,000 years, the action of these two sources of water here is significant. With an average rainfall rate of only 2.5cms per year, the sphinx would have still been exposed over five millennia, to about 91.5m (300 ft) of rainfall during its existence! Limestone slowly dissolves when exposed to water, especially soft limestone. But in fact, in addition, severe storms can dump a lot of water onto the Giza plateau, causing heavy run-off. And since the limestone was originally long ages ago under the waters of an ancient ocean, its salt content becomes very corrosive when the rainwater moistens the rock.

So, what is the truth here? Schoch has received support for his conclusion from some other geologists, but these geologists may not have been informed as to the complex layering of the huge sphinx, and the topography of the Giza plateau. The sphinx is actually composed of three different kinds of limestone, and the middle section, where the erosion can easily be seen, is made of a very soft limestone which erodes easily from exposure to moisture or wind or sandstorms or accumulated moisture in the sand. We shall make a clear decision about this, and re-visit the theme of water erosion after we have examined the other evidence as to its age.

The Meaning of the Sphinx; what does it symbolize?
Trying to establish the age of the sphinx takes one right into a confusing circle. We need to consider what its meaning may be, for this would lead us to discover its age, but the reverse is also true: we can discover the meaning of the sphinx, once we know its age, the culture from which it derives. However, as we have seen, there are very opposing views as to how old it is, because people's conclusion about its age is linked to their view of its meaning! So, how do we find our way out of the maze? Lets start by looking at the symbolism of this strange mythical beast, and then consider the latest archaeological research. In contrast to most other sphinxes from antiquity, and there are many, the one at Giza is actually a lion with a human head.

Now, this is very important, because the classical idea of a sphinx is not like this, it is made up of lion talons, eagle wings, bull torso and, rising up above all this, a human head. This fourfold symbolic form was prominent in ancient Mesopotamia; and later it was taken up strongly in esoteric Greek circles, and it has a place in both Jewish and Christian mystical teachings. The classical fourfold sphinx obviously resonated deeply as a symbol of some profound truth with many diverse peoples.

Researchers into sacred symbols conclude that the classical sphinx which originates in Mesopotamia, represents a primary theme in spirituality: the arising of the human heart and mind over the animal kingdom.[5] More specifically, it appears that to the ancients, these three animal species, the feline (lion), bird (eagle) and ruminant (bull) represent the most fundamental and primordial strands of animal life and thus consciousness of living beings on the Earth. They are like the three bases from which all the other animals have derived. So, the classical sphinx was a depiction of unconquered, lower energies lurking in the soul; hence it represents a negative quality. Ancient Assyrian carvings show this composite creature.[6] The sphinx acted as a threat to those seeking spirituality. One could say that it symbolized the lower self within; indeed the name we use for this symbolic creature comes from Greek and means the strangler. This negative view of the classic sphinx is depicted in Greek myths, and is found in Freemason literature and in the famous drama, *Faust*, written by Johannes W. von Goethe.

The classic sphinx is then a symbol of the great drama of humanity's long struggle to rise above these animal energies, and to find a higher, truly human nature. It was exactly this ethical spiritual challenge, especially the mystical side of it, rising up to a spiritual re-birth, which was the focus of the ancient Mysteries. This means that when the acolyte in the Mysteries encountered the imperfections in their soul (the so-called lower self), it would be a somewhat suffocating, disempowering experience.

Statues of this true fourfold sphinx were used outside sacred sites, where they were thought of as guardians. Not because they are good beings, but because in representing a spiritually real lower self they warn the curious soul not to try to enter into the sacred realm without due preparation, i.e., without having conquered the lower drives. It also happened that such a menacing form was used at times to guard burial places, in

---

[5] J. C. Cooper, Illustrated Encyclopedia of Symbols, Thames & Hudson, London,1978, R. Steiner, Egyptian myths and Mysteries, 1908.
[6] see websites www.ferrelljenkins.files.wordpress.com/2007/05/ and http://www.talariaenterprises.com/images2/3529b.jpg

the belief that intruders would be scared off by it. The true sphinx, a strange and unpleasant creature, does not come from Egypt.

The Egyptians never carved this classical sphinx; all the sphinxes from Egypt are in fact lion-bodied, human headed forms.[7] Since the lion is a symbol of the sun, the Egyptian sphinx is a representation of the sun, on a spiritual level; we could say it represents sun beings, or spiritual solar energies, if you wish. It was the case in medieval and Hellenistic times that lions, more than other animals, were thought of as inwardly linked to the sun's spiritual energies. Hence the lion is a symbol of the sun in various ancient systems of mystical thought. The lion is the royal beast, who represents the royal star, the sun; and it is very likely that this same view held sway in the Old Kingdom of Egypt.

And the sun is the monarch that rules over the other stars of our solar system, since of course they are only planets. It has nothing to do with the lower aspect of the personality and the three primary animal qualities, which the classical sphinx depicts. The Egyptian sphinx, as carved at Giza, and all later sphinxes from Egypt, have this leonine-human form, indicating noble spiritual qualities. This is known from texts which call the sphinx Harmakhis or Horus-in-the-Horizon. These names refer to a god who is an aspect of the great sun god, called Ra (or Osiris). This Egyptian sphinx could be placed outside a site sacred to the sun god, as an indicator of the sacredness of the site.

So summing up, at Giza there is not a classical sphinx, but a human-headed lion sphinx form. This leonine-human form symbolizes divine spirit beings, specifically sun spirits. So there is a striking difference between the Egyptian sphinx and the full fourfold classical sphinx. To the ancients, the full sphinx depicted the various animal strands, and these are indeed lowly energies – especially when compared to, or

---

[7] There are a few depictions of griffins in later Egyptian art, which vaguely resemble a sphinx.

intruding into, human consciousness. But in their own right, not when active inside the human soul, ancient people experienced animals as a valid spiritual reality; they viewed them as deriving from what we today call God.

Although the three primary animal groups are lowly in comparison to the human, if they are considered spiritually, then they are seen as each having a kind of over-soul, a spiritual being of majesty and validity. In that sense the animals' over-soul was revered. And this is the case with the Egyptian leonine sphinx. But can we get more understanding of what the sphinx symbolized? Yes, from the carved stele (an inscribed upright stone slab) which exists between the paws of the sphinx; set up by the pharaoh Thothmes IV.

The Stele of Thothmes IV: the sphinx and the sun god
This stele has a reference to two deities, known as the Akeru. The Akeru is a dual deity, depicted as two lions in the form of two sphinxes, not human-headed lions. This symbol represents the influence of the setting and the rising sun. So the Akeru is closely linked to the leonine sphinx (Ra-Harmakhis), and explains its meaning. The sphinx symbolizes the sun god, and the Akeru lions depicted on the stele between its paws, represent the setting and rising of the sun god. Thothmes IV reigned from about 1447 to 1438 BC, some 1,200 years after Khafre who is regarded as the builder of the sphinx.

Thothmes tells how during a hunting trip he rested from the midday heat in the vicinity of the sphinx, and then had a special dream or vision in which a great divine being, whom the sphinx represents, appeared to him. This being was called Heru-khuti or Horakhty (in Greek, Ra-Harmakhis), which means, Horus-of-the-Horizon(s), a deity who is an aspect of the sun god Ra. This deity appealed to the Pharaoh to rescue his own image, i.e., the carved sphinx, from the encroaching sand. The following is a part of the inscription:

> ....Then came his (Thothmes IV) time for allowing rest to his servants, at a locality consecrated to the gods, {i.e., to

19

the deity, Harmakhis or Horus-in-the-Horizon} a locality sacred to the god Sokaris {a form of Osiris}, in The Necropolis {i.e., the Giza plateau}....(which is}...at that sacred place of the creation, which......is the sacred path of the gods towards the western horizon of On (the city of Heliopolis).
For the sphinx (the image of Khopri), the very Mighty, resides in this place.......
A dreamlike vision seized the pharaoh at the hour (when) the sun was in the zenith, and he found the majesty of this revered god speaking with his own mouth, as a father speaks with his son, saying: "Behold thou me! See thou me! My son Thutmose, I am thy father, Harmakhis-Khepri-Re-Atum, who will give to thee my kingdom on Earth at the head of the living. Thou shalt wear the white crown and the red crown upon the throne of Keb, the hereditary prince.... Behold my actual condition that thou mayest protect all my perfect limbs. The sand of the desert whereon I am laid has covered me....[4]

We can learn many things from this invaluable, if wordy, text. The long name of the sphinx, Harmakhis-Khepri-Ra-Atum means literally "Horus-in-the-horizon-sun God-father God". In other words, the sphinx is the sun god as he appears on the Earth, rising and setting, and is therefore also part of the actual sun god (Ra) and yet it is also linked to the great father God, the Creator, Atum. His spirit has spoken to the pharaoh in a psychic experience, and asked him to remove the sand from its body. But, from this we learn that the sphinx was regarded as a symbol of the spiritual energies or deities, associated with the sun; perhaps one could say, it symbolized a spiritual sun, not the physical sun.

So, the human-headed lion figure crouching on the Giza plateau represents the sun or rather those spiritual beings associated with the sun, Ra and Horus, themselves being an expression of the higher Father-God figure called Atum. It is as if a variety of solar beings were perceived by the ancient Egyptians behind the physical sun, so to speak. So, the

Egyptian sphinx represents in particular Harmakhis, who is an aspect of the sun god Ra. And as associated gods there are the Akeru, representing Ra's importance for the Earth and its inhabitants, through his setting and rising.

The link between the sphinx and the sun god is confirmed further in the text inscribed by pharaoh Thothmes IV. The Pharaoh goes on to say more about this link,

> "...the sphinx, Ra-Harmakhis {represents} the life of the universal Lord (the sun), and is protected by Atum... {he is on} the sacred path of the gods towards the western horizon of Annu (Heliopolis); for the sphinx of Khopri, the very mighty, resides in this place..." [4]

In other words, the sphinx is a representative of the sun god, and he is also linked to Atum, the uncaused great God, but the sphinx is also linked to the sacred site of the sun god worship, the town of Heliopolis. This town, with its temple and its priesthood dedicated to the sun god, was the foremost centre of the Egyptian sun religion. The god Atum is in effect what is called God today, i.e., the primeval creator-god, and Ra-Harmakhis, representing the sun god, is the representation of this cosmic creator at a more discernible level, namely of the sun's powers.

This tablet tells us that behind this impetus to create the sphinx, and to restore it 1,200 years later, was the influence of the priesthood of the sacred town of Heliopolis, the site of the sun god cult. Heliopolis was about 25kms northeast of the Giza plateau. The god Atum was worshipped at Heliopolis since time immemorial, but gradually the mysteries of the sun god, symbolized by the sphinx, became the focus of the priesthood and their Mysteries.

Chapter Two: the Sphinx and the spiritual sun-disc

Heliopolis, and the sun sentinel Ra-Harmakhis

Now, since the Egyptian religion in historical times was very much focussed on the worship of this spiritual-sun or the sun spirit, this is a strong, but not yet an absolute, indicator that mainstream conclusions about the age of the sphinx are correct. Namely, that the sphinx was carved about 2,800 - 2,600 BC, that is during the Egyptian Old Kingdom, and it represents Ra-Harmakhis or Heru-khuti, or Horus-in-the-Horizon.

Its huge, mute presence reminds people of this aspect of the sun god, and this is an important task in ancient Egyptian beliefs, for both the living and the dead. The sphinx on the Giza plateau is illumined at sunrise, because it is directly facing the sun god Ra-Horus. At sunrise, it lights up as the rays of the sun spread out above it, filling the eastern horizon. And if you are near the Sphinx in the later summer months when Sirius is so prominent, the setting sun descends below the north-western horizon.

The north-western sunset point is then located in between the two huge pyramids of Khufu and Khafre, they are like two mountains on either side of it. But this situation creates the hieroglyph for horizon: the sun between two mountains! This then, is part of the integrated design plan for the Giza plateau, and is the site chosen for the great human-headed lion, the representative of Horus-in-the-Horizon, who is often referred to in ancient hieroglyphics texts as being both the rising and the setting sun.

The core of the Egyptian religious life was the reverence of the sun god, called Ra or Osiris; and the human-headed lion body sphinx was a symbol of this. But perhaps we have still not been able to dismiss the idea that the sphinx was carved by some pre-diluvial Egyptian civilization, which also worshipped sun spirits. So, now that we understand the meaning of the sphinx, can we find out its true age?

The Age of the Sphinx and the rising of Sirius
The ancient Egyptians associated the sun (Ra or his intermediary Horus) with the zodiac stars, in particular Taurus; many statues and texts refer to Horus as the powerful Bull. For example the three obelisks that were taken away from Egypt about 200 years ago and set up in New York, London and Paris, all have inscriptions revering the sun god, the great bull. These all came from Heliopolis, and were originally set up there by Thothmes IV. That the sun is called the powerful Bull indicates that it is associated with the zodiac constellation of Taurus.

But if one goes back in time looking for zodiacal era in which the sun rose in a particular constellation at the spring equinox, one finds out that the sun was in Leo the lion about 10,000 BC. So the question arises, why is the lion used to represent the sun god in this statue of the sphinx, instead of a bull, if it truly is from the Old Kingdom, when the sun was in Taurus the Bull every springtime? If it were pre-diluvial, that is built before the Great Flood, perhaps in the fabled Atlantean Age or whatever, then it would indeed be a lion shaped statue. But if it is only about 5,000 years old, why not have the sacred bull as the sun symbol; why have a lion?

We can give two answers here, confirming the experts' view that the sphinx is from the Old Kingdom of Egypt, and not pre-diluvial. Firstly as we have seen, the primary reason for the lion shape is that this great carving represents the sun spirit, whose earthly representative is the lion. The second contributing factor to the decision by the Heliopolitan priests to carve a lion and not a bull, even though it was carved in the zodiacal age of the Bull, has to do with the position of the sun at the beginning of summer, when the New Year began for the ancient Egyptians. Their New Year was the summer solstice, not the springtime, and this was a time when the brilliant star Sirius reappeared over the horizon.

This powerful star, the most brilliant of all stars in the night sky, was very important to their religious life and rituals, it was regarded spiritually as a sister sun to the sun of our solar system, so to speak. And in terms of practical external life, every year shortly after the summer solstice, Sirius reappeared over the horizon of the night sky, after months of being below the horizon. This coincided with beginning of the time each year that the river Nile began to flood over its banks.

This flooding brought great quantities of rich silt, making Egyptian agriculture productive, and hence civilized life itself possible to the peoples of the Nile. Now at the time of the Old Kingdom, about the same time of the year when Sirius rose over the eastern horizon, the sun shone down from the constellation of Leo the lion.

The Leonine summer warmth and the rich silt from the Nile river inaugurated the new cycle of fertility for the land. So, speaking in terms of the holistic view of ancient peoples, and remembering that this great monument directly faces the rising sun in the east, the lion-bodied sphinx mutely speaks of the power of the Leo energies intermingled with the Sun's energies, at that time when Sirius re-appears. This is what the ancient Egyptians experienced: at dawn, as the twilight glow of the sun began, Sirius could be seen rising, whilst the sun in the constellation of Leo, illumined the great sphinx.

And this is in the summertime; solar energies which bestow life on Earth intensify amidst the pre-dawn stars of Leo, and also early in those early summer mornings the great star-sun Sirius reappears. And in those same weeks when Sirius reappears, the Nile River floods, bringing life-renewing water to the parched land. It was as if this re-appearing of Sirius gave life-renewing fertility to the whole land; and this very process echoes the life-bestowing powers of the sun god itself. Fertility was connected to the sun in the minds of ancient people.

Hence the solar energies intermingled with Leo in July, conjoined with those from Sirius's life-giving reappearance, becoming central to the life experience of the ancient Egyptians of the Old Kingdom. This view was also the conclusion of a Greek initiate from the first century AD, called Plutarch; a high priest at the world-famous sanctuary of Apollo at Delphi. In his treatise on Isis and Osiris, Plutarch writes about the association of the sun, Sirius and Leo in the thinking of the Egyptian priests,[8]

> ...of the stars, Sirius is consecrated to Isis, for this star is the one that brings the water (of the Nile onto the land). Also the Egyptians revere the lion, and adorn the doors of their temples with open-jawed lions, because the Nile overflows after the sun first unites with the lion (Leo).[9] (Author's trans.)

One sees here in this 2,000-year-old text from a priest of the Grecian Mysteries, how there is a feeling for subtle energies affecting the Earth from the cosmos, and for the interaction between these two. This attitude was probably more potent still, some 3,000 years earlier than Plutarch.

The true age of the Sphinx
Egyptologists, quoting statements actually found in old Egyptian texts, maintain that Pharaoh Khufu built the Great Pyramid, and that then Khafre, the son of Khufu, built the second pyramid, and the great sphinx, too. However, the alternative New Age view is that not only the sphinx but also all three great Giza pyramids were built by an unknown civilisation many millennia before Khafre (perhaps in so-called Atlantean times). We have seen some strong reason to doubt this pre-diluvial dating of the sphinx, but what solid evidence is there to show that the sphinx was carved at the time of Khafre, or perhaps 100-200 years earlier?

---

[8] ΠΛΟΥΤΑΡΧΟΥ ΠΕΡΙ ΙΣΔΟΣ ΚΑΙ ΟΣΙΡΙΔΟΣ, edit. G. Parthey, Nicolaische Buchhandlung, Berlin, 1850 p. 65.
[9] The Greek: Τῶν τε ἄστρων τὸν σείρον Ἴσιδος νομίζουσιν, ὑδραγωγὸν ὄντα· καὶ τὸν λέοντα τιμῶσι, καὶ χάσμασι λεοντείοις τὰ τῶν ἱερων θυρώματα κοσμοῦσί, ὅτι πλημμυρῖ Νεῖλος

An authority in Egyptian archaeology, Mark Lehner, under the leadership of Dr. Hawass (Secretary General of the Supreme Council of Antiquities for many years), has pointed out that excavations around and even inside the sphinx (in deep crevices formed naturally in its body) has led to discoveries of fragments of pottery and tools, **lodged in deeper layers of the sphinx itself. And these artefacts in fact date from the Old Kingdom.** Dr. Lehner is not a narrow-minded authority; some years ago, he did take seriously the fascinating statements of the American trance medium Edgar Cayce, who said that the Giza monuments go back long into pre-diluvial times.[10] But the actual evidence of the site itself has convinced Lehner that Cayce is wrong.

That these artefacts were found in the grand causeway of Khafre, and deep inside the sphinx itself, constitutes irrefutable evidence of a specific date of construction. That date is the Old Kingdom era of Egypt; in the era when the pharaoh Khufu and Khafre reigned. No specific proof has been found to link Khafre to the sphinx (except a computer reconstruction of the damaged face which is very like that of Khafre), but certainly it can be linked to the Old Kingdom.

Secondly, other evidence exists which shows that the sphinx was constructed at the same time as the second pyramid, the one associated with Khafre. It should also be borne in mind that this question needs to be contemplated in the over-all context of the site, namely the relation of the sphinx to other features on the Giza plateau. From the diagram, [illustration 1] you can see that there is a causeway from the Sphinx Temple, alongside the sphinx up to the second pyramid, it is known as Khafre's causeway. This causeway is exactly parallel to the angled wall of the enclosure for the Sphinx, which it runs along.

The two structures were obviously constructed at the same time, the angled causeway is quite organic to its site and to the

---

[10] Lehner compiled Cayce's Egyptian readings into a book "The Egyptian Heritage" in 1974 (ARE Press).

neighbouring monument, and this parallelism is not a coincidence.[11]

Even if the two monuments were constructed one or two centuries earlier, if it is the case that Khafre's reign was actually 100-200 years earlier than now thought, the sphinx and the second pyramid are certainly not 10,000 years old, for they were constructed in the Old Kingdom. We also need to note now the presence of other buildings associated with the sphinx. These are Khafre's Valley Temple, and the Sphinx Temple, both of which are an integral part of the sphinx's purpose. The front and back of both temples are nearly aligned, and they are situated on the same terrace, below and a little to the east of the Sphinx.

This also creates a solid reason to date them together with the sphinx, and they also are very similar in their layout. We shall consider Khafre's Valley Temple later, as it is designed primarily to service the after-life needs of the pharaoh. But what about the extent of the weathering of the sphinx? Doesn't it show signs of being subject to **water** erosion, which has to mean that it was carved many millennia ago in some pre-diluvial age?

The weathering of the Sphinx
We noted earlier that arguments have been put forward to the effect that the severe weathering of the sphinx is due to water exposure, and not exposure to sand erosion, and so its severe erosion was not caused by strong sandstorms driving sand against it. And therefore this water erosion, so the argument says, must have been brought about by floods, in a time before the fertile Saharan plains became the dry desert of today. But as we noted earlier, this idea has been strongly countered by the fact that the sphinx has a middle section of soft limestone, and has been exposed to about an accumulated 100 metres of rainwater run-off over about 5,000 years.

---

[11] For more excellent data about the Khafre-Sphinx link, see the article by Z. Hawass at www.gizapyramids.org

Further arguments against the extreme age theory of the sphinx, as put forward by Schoch, are provided by other expert geologists, such as J. A. Harrell March and August Matthusen. March explains that in the 400 metre causeway alongside the sphinx, from Khafre's pyramid to his Valley Temple, there exist really substantial drainage channels, and these are obviously designed to carry substantial run-off of rainwater away from the limestone monuments. Now for several thousand years, the body of the sphinx was covered in accumulated sand.

It was only briefly cleared of the sand after 1,200 years by Pharaoh Thothmes IV, and not again for some 3,000 years, in the 19th century restoration projects. During this time rainfall will have resulted in water accumulating in the sand and covering much of the sphinx, and this accumulated moisture, activating the salt crystals, could stay for weeks or months. This has happened every year for about 5,000 years, gradually eroding the soft middle section of the monument.

Moreover, very importantly, the sphinx is actually sited in the lower area of the Giza plateau. So, if we only consider the usual scanty rainfall of this area, leaving aside the occasional heavy thunderstorm, the rainwater will accumulate around it, because any surface run-off, as well as seepage of water underneath the sand, will drain down to where the sphinx is, and then down into the Nile. So, the 100 metres of precipitated rain becomes something like 300 metres in real terms. In fact in the 1980's, when the sand around the sphinx was once again cleared away, it was reported to be completely soaked with water; see March's website.[12] And at least one of the clay brick minor pyramids on the Giza Plateau has been seriously damaged from heavy rain during severe storms, in the last two millennia.

However, the persistent Schoch refers to another limestone monument, dating from the Old Kingdom, not far from the

---

[12] www.geology.utoledo.edu/research/archaeology)

sphinx, and points out that it is really not so weathered, despite being also subject to accumulated moisture. But as Larry Orcutt explains, Schoch omits to say that it is composed of a different type of limestone, a very hard type, which will not be weathered as easily as the middle section of the sphinx. It is also on a higher part of the plateau, and therefore has not been subject to sand-drift nor accumulated water. See his website, for clear refutations of the theory of the extreme age of the sphinx.[13]

So the argument that the sphinx is about 10,000 years old is quite wrong. It has been subject to more substantial rain runoff than normally realized, it is an integral part of a well-designed over-all siting of other monuments, which are known to date from the Old Kingdom, and finally, Old Kingdom artefacts have been found deep inside its body, from the time when it was being carved. However, it is not impossible that the sphinx is just one or two centuries older than the currently accepted 4,600 years.

Indeed Rainer Stadelmann, a world authority on the Giza plateau, has concluded that the evidence linking the sphinx specifically with Khafre is so slight that, although it does belong to the Old Kingdom period, it may have been built by Khufu, a few decades before. We shall consider the dating again when we explore the controversy and alternative ideas about the age of the Great Pyramid.[14] We now should briefly note the Sphinx Temple, which like the sphinx, also was designed to serve the religious-spiritual needs of the people, quite apart from the after-life needs.

The Sphinx Temple
In front of the sphinx is the Temple of the Sphinx, which was once open to the sky, and had a central court some 46 metres long (151 ft) and 2.5m (10 ft) wide, surrounded by high walls.

---

[13] www.catchpenny.org/sphinx

[14] One reason the earlier date is preferred in alternative circles is that Madam Blavatsky, the founder of the Theosophical Society (founded 1875) said that it went back into "early Atlantean times".

From inside, it would have offered an excellent view of the front of the great sphinx. The Sphinx Temple was built on a terrace about 2m (6.6ft) lower than the sphinx itself. The court was paved with white alabaster, and was replete with tall pillars and various recesses. This ancient temple was unique in having not one, but two sanctuaries; one in the eastern side, the other in the western side. And, like the sphinx, it is aligned east-west. Thus both the rising sun and the setting sun could be experienced from it.

In other words, here we have an indication that this temple was dedicated to the sun god Ra, in his form as Harmakhis, the sphinx, who rises and sets each day; and these two sanctuaries also indicate that the Akeru are implied. So, again we see that the human-headed lion carved on Giza expresses reverence of the sun (i.e., the sun god), hence it faces the rising sun, and its associated temple facilitated the cult of the sun god. But in addition, archaeological research has established that this temple once had 12 statues and 24 columns; and this is very suggestive of a focus on some larger, celestial theme. It could have been the solar year with possibly a zodiac influence, or the solar year as a larger version of a 24 hour day.

So these ritual functions are all entirely appropriate to the Old Kingdom of Egypt, and also organically emerge from the culture and architecture of that period. There is no need, and indeed it is quite artificial, to date this temple or the sphinx, to the time of an "Atlantean" Age of Leo (ca. 9,000 BC). But now it is becoming evident that the Giza plateau was not just a necropolis, it was also a religious or spiritual site for the everyday religious needs of the people.

Some of its temples and monuments were designed to facilitate other needs of the cultural life, quite apart from the needs of the dead in the after-life. The sphinx and its temples are of this sort; they were part of a spiritual-religious cult revering the sun god. The great sphinx is one feature amongst others, which show us that the second aspect of the Giza Plateau; a site for religious-spiritual purposes.

The Sphinx, secret chambers and tunnels?

In sensational literature and websites concerning the Giza plateau, rumours circulate about tunnels and chambers underneath the sphinx, which are being kept secret. This fascination has been fuelled by the prophecies of Edgar Cayce, who made various statements about important underground tunnels here. Extensive research has been undertaken by scientific teams and serious amateur researchers using ground-penetrating radar, etc. And these people have indeed detected what appear to be chambers, and even tunnels. However, the chambers have to be regarded as just normal limestone cavities until they are visually inspected; then one or two might be confirmed as ancient chambers of cultural significance.

Dr. Hawass reports that these have not yet been inspected; presumably because he has concluded that they are just natural hollows in the limestone, and hence of little value. As to the tunnels, Dr. Hawass reports that these have been inspected, and they do not go anywhere, they are usually quite short, and hence of no interest. One of these tunnels he reports, is 45 ft long and extends in the direction of the pyramid of Khafre, but then it just terminates, serving no known purpose. But it is still possible that there is a chamber underneath the sphinx, that was used for sacred rituals or even storage of ancient documents. The discovery of a museum-library type chamber of this kind would indeed be a colossal archaeological discovery, and it may happen in future times.

Ra-Harmakhis: The spiritual sun-disc and its worship

A study of the graphic images and writings left behind by earlier cultures indicates that humanity in those earlier ages experienced the cosmos as en-souled, so to speak. It is obvious that there was some kind of holistic consciousness within earlier cultures and eras. That is, to earlier peoples, behind the molecules of the material world was a realm of energies and also realms of spiritual beings. They saw the universe as more than just a physical, molecular object; many spirit beings inhabited it. This view went in parallel with their holistic view of the human being, who also had, apart from the physical body, a subtle life-force and a soul, and there were also several other parts to this soul, and there was a spiritual aspect as well. The exact relationship of these various elements of a person to what we call the soul (or consciousness) is not described in the literature, but it is clear that each human being consisted of a multiple of elements.

In Egypt for example, the human being consisted of the Khat (physical body), the Ba or Sekhem (apparently the life-force), the Ka (a kind of soul which has a sentient capacity), the Akh, (or akhu, khu, ikhu) this is the seat of intelligence. And there were still other elements as well. But in antiquity, this same multi-layered view was also applied to the planets and the stars, the sun was not only a ball of energy existing on the physical plane; there was a spiritual level to it, great spirit beings were associated with this level.

The ancients believed that these other levels of creation, beyond molecular substance, could be perceived. It was also pivotal in old religions that the will of the gods could be made known by the spiritual processes carried out by the priests or priestesses. And this was the purpose behind the complex religious and initiatory systems instituted in earlier ages.

Each planet and the sun had an indwelling spiritual being, and these were called the planetary Intelligence or the spirit of each planet; by the Hellenistic era they were given specific names. The spirit of the sun was a much greater divinity than the planetary spirits, just as the sun is physically greater than the planets. This view that the sun has a great spiritual reality behind its physical form was a doctrine in the Hellenistic Mystery cults and it survived into the first centuries of the Christian era, through the cult of Mithra.

In 316 AD the new Christian emperor, Julian the Apostate, was initiated into the Mithraic cult, and he wrote a treatise about the triune sun. He viewed the sun as existing, firstly, on a high transcendental level, and secondly on a less transcendent soul level where it is worshipped as Helios or Mithra and was associated with hosts of angelic beings, and thirdly, as the visible sun disc.

So, how can we relate to these ideas about a multi-level cosmos, and thus appreciate the Giza plateau monuments more fully? Modern astronomy teaches that the Earth was cast out of the sun long ages ago, and when this occurred, the Earth was just a fiery, vaporous ball of gases and dust. If one were to bring this modern view to Egyptian priests from long ago, they would probably comment that, in addition to the dust and gaseous matter, some kind of subtle life-force was already there in the Earth at that remote time too.

And moreover, this subtle life-force now permeates the atmosphere and animates every living cell of our planet, because the primordial Earth, in being cast out of the parent body, the Sun, took with it its own share of these higher energies too. This idea is traceable in some of the ancient creation myths, where mention is made of how the upper world (heaven) is wrenched up and way from the lower world (the Earth), but this lower world of ours retained a share of the multi-level creation.

Moreover, an ancient Egyptian priest probably would say that all this has real implications for the Earth, because it means that the sun is the originating body from which the Earth and humanity came. It was not just the gaseous, fiery physical body, which was cast out of the sun, but also the higher, subtle elements of the human being, such as the soul. And this meant to the ancients that the spirit-beings of the sun are the creators of the Earth and of humanity, not only in a physical sense, but also on a soul level.

This is perhaps the inner reason why the ancients developed a cult of sun worship. From their viewpoint, to revere the sun meant to revere the spiritual deities who are behind its physical form, and from whom the Earth and its many life-waves owe their existence. Of course in early communities where the beginnings of the agricultural work was developed, the role of the sun in the seasonal cycle, and in the maturing of the crops, was very significant.

A study of the religious texts involved in the worship of the sun indicates that this was common religious behaviour; it was a revering of the creator. It was what we call worshipping God, as the creator of the Earth and humanity. But in the unusual sense that the sun was seen as the originator of our physical planet and all the souls who live here. Hence if a person has a soul or an even higher aspect, a spiritual part, then this has its origin in the sun spirit too.

Today scientifically the sun is also seen as the originator of the planet; but the planet as only a physical-material thing. However, it's worth remembering that the view of creation is changing enormously because of astronomical research. About a century ago the astronomical view was that the sun was simply a hot ball of gas and some visible light rays; but all of this has changed since the development of radio-astronomy. This branch of science registers electronically, or as images on special film various levels of radiation, of strange invisible energies, streaming out from the sun (or from elsewhere in space).

In the development of modern materialism, during the 18th and 19th centuries, the centuries-old Christian view of God, (and belief in astrological influences, etc.) died out. It was replaced by the conviction that out there was a void, permeated only by the forces of gravity. These physical forces became the force that made the solar system function. But in the mid-twentieth century, as the capacity developed to register invisible energies electronically, the spiritual element began to flow back in, at least in the rudimentary form of energies within the electro-magnetic spectrum.

So now we don't just have the physical sun, but there are at least six levels to the sun out there. That is, the sun has various states of being, or levels of existence, each of which is a spherical body or glowing 'sun' in its own right, raying out energies. A website to see images of these various suns is: http://www.solar.physics.montana.edu/ypop/Spotlight/Today.

It is clear from ancient creation stories, that to the early priesthoods, spiritual beings within the spiritual sun specifically arranged for the creation of the Earth and humanity, and imbued the planet's eco-system with its wisdom and natural laws. A modern religious person would object by saying, this sounds reasonable perhaps when it is put into its original context, but surely the actual Creator is a great being; a being beyond the sun, indeed beyond everything in material creation.

It appears that the ancient priests of the sun god would have agreed to this conclusion; for as we have seen, they also had a greater, uncaused God beyond the sun. His (or its) name was Atum (or Tum or Tem). As we noted earlier, this deity created Ra the sun god, and was involved in the primordial act of creation.

At Heliopolis in the upper Nile delta, the town of the sun god where the worship of Ra and Harmakhis (represented by the sphinx) originated, the cult of Atum was a primary element of the religious life. The great Atum is described as the maker of the Khu, the spark of intelligence in our soul. Our Khu or higher intelligence is described in a wonderful poetic image, as "coming into being from the eyelashes of Atem".[15]

The great yearning of the ancient Egyptians was that after death they would be able to arise into the realm of the sun, on a spiritual level. They called it the kingdom of Ra (or Osiris). Helping them to achieve this goal was Horus, who was an intermediary between the sun god and humanity. It is therefore obvious that in the Old Kingdom religious rituals were held in the Sphinx Temple to facilitate the goal of being attuned to the sun god, and finding the way to his realm.

---

[15] E. A. Wallis-Budge, The Egyptian Book of the Dead, chapter 78, RKP, London, 1969, p. 252.

So far, we have explored two monuments that are designed for use in the general religious or spiritual life of the culture and its priests; the Sphinx and the Sphinx Temple. And it is important to note that these monuments are not exclusively designed for the souls of the dead. They are part of the second aspect of the Giza plateau: a general religious site for carrying out rituals to worship the gods.

Conclusions: the true age and the significance of the great Sphinx

The great sphinx was carved in, or a little before, the reign of Khafre, about 2,700 BC, as a symbol of the great sun god Ra, the god whom the ancient Egyptians revered for several reasons. He brought life and fertility to the Earth, but he also provided light for the souls of the dead. It was into his realm after death that the Egyptian so deeply yearned to enter, and not be impeded by the evil serpent, Apep.

Various ancient texts highlight this dire need, such as the Book of the Amduat and The Book of the Dead, showing that it was a dire necessity for the deceased on his journey that he or she accomplish this. As we shall see, a careful re-examination of ancient Egyptian texts by expert Egyptologists reveal that it was also this realm that the priests sought to reach in their spiritual experiences.

The god of this realm is represented by the sphinx, called Ra-Harmakhis. The implication of these old writings, and the main Creation myth itself, is that our Earth came into being from the spiritual level of the sun, and the human soul strives up to the radiant realm of the sun spirit, upon entering the after-life. The reverence of the sun spirit is a theme that is found again and again in exploring ancient sacred sites anywhere. So far we have seen two monuments which, although associated with the after-life, are also focussed on the religious-spiritual themes of the times.

Chapter Three: The Great Pyramid

The first riddle: moving huge stone slabs

We will now consider the Great Pyramid and see whether it was only a tomb or a place designed for the religious-spiritual life of the ancient Egyptians; or both these functions together. The Great Pyramid is of course the most extraordinary monument here, and indeed worldwide it is without equal, for many reasons. So we shall devote a substantial space to our exploration of this monument.

When many ancient monuments in sacred sites across the world are carefully examined, it is a striking fact that the construction of them is sometimes found to be an extraordinary engineering feat. In some sites the construction of a monument appears to be far beyond the capacity of the early civilization which built it; leading to all sorts of speculation. Many of the ancient sites could perhaps have been built with ingenious use of primitive surveying techniques and astronomical observations, as well as ramps or pulley systems, and lots of muscle power. And this is certainly partly true of the monuments here on the Giza plateau.

It is important not to under-estimate what skills and persistence and muscle-power of people can achieve, when the construction of a sacred site is called for by an ancient priesthood. However the sheer size and weight of the huge stone slabs used in the Great Pyramid, and then fitting them together with such extraordinary accuracy, does seem to point to a form of technology unknown to us today. There are other features to the Great Pyramid that likewise seem to point to the involvement of an unknown technology. And as we shall see, in some instances it appears that just possibly a mental faculty unknown to us today, was involved.

The method of construction of the Great Pyramid and the sphinx has been subject to extensive research projects, precisely because it is difficult for science to explain how they could have been built. In the late 1990's for example, a project was undertaken to examine the technical challenges involved in building the sphinx true to scale, within its enclosure. It showed clearly that, despite using the largest cranes in the world today, modern machinery could not re-create some of these ancient Egyptian monuments. The huge cranes cannot manoeuvre such huge weights in the confined space allowed. Some of the stone slabs used on the Giza plateau weigh an estimated 200 tonnes, and one of them weighs some 468 tonnes.[16]

This point about the moving of large stone slabs is very relevant, especially to the Great Pyramid, which is a huge monument; standing near it makes you feel truly just a tiny ant-like being. It covers some thirteen acres, or 5.26 hectares, equal to four city blocks in size. Consisting of about two and a half million blocks of stone, each weighing between two and seventy tonnes, it is considered the largest building ever constructed. Even elementary facts about the engineering capabilities needed to construct the Great Pyramid are intriguing, to say the least.

The original site, a rock hill, had to be substantially reduced before the pyramid was constructed over it; and although it covers such a huge area, its base is incredibly level. The unevenness from one side to the other is less than one inch (2.1cm)! For more about the technical difficulties of building the Great Pyramid and various theories on this, see the Appendix.

Another intriguing point about the uncanny capacity of the ancient builders concerns the accuracy of the construction of an internal feature; this is known as the Descending Passage. This is a narrow tunnel which goes down 350 ft (107 m) into the dark depths of the huge monument's base, where it terminates in a mysterious, roughly hewn chamber of no known use, but of potent symbolic meaning. Surveying of this

---

[16] website: google keyword: .Mars Hill symposium

tunnel reveals that it deviates from being perfectly straight, from one end to the other, by less than ¼ inch (6mm) in the sides, and only 3/10 inch (.76cm) in the ceiling! This aspect alone is astonishing, considering that the tunnel is only 3'11" (1.19 m) in height, which prevented the workmen from ever standing up, whilst hewing their way with soft copper tools (?) through solid rock, in a darkness alleviated only by pitch torches. It is astonishing not only for the technical skill implied, but because it again makes us ask the question, "Why?" Why would the high priests have insisted on such an accurate engineering achievement? But this is a question which can be asked of the entire internal structure, and positioning of the Great Pyramid.

False and misleading rumours about the Great Pyramid
Some nonsense facts have been claimed for this monument. It is said for example, that the internal dimensions of the mysterious sarcophagus in the upper chamber, are exactly the same as the fabled Ark of the Covenant. This is quite simply nonsense; the two objects have completely different dimensions. The Great Pyramid has also been described as containing a secret mathematical or geometrical code inside it, i.e., embedded in its measurements, which is a kind of cipher, and contains prophecies about the future.

For example, it is claimed that knowledge of these codes allows one to know the apocalyptic secrets of the future, such as the date of the return of Jesus, or the date of the commencement of World War II. These claims are not a 20th century phenomenon; it was already in full swing in the mid 19th century. Some of this excitement derives from 19th century religious people, with a narrow approach to the Bible, such as Charles Piazzi Smith.

Smith decided that the builders had incorporated an ancient measurement, which he called the pyramid inch or the sacred cubit, in the dimensions of the pyramid. This sacred cubit turns out to be almost the same as the British inch, in length! This conclusion reflects his Biblical belief that some of the lost tribes of Israel were once in Egypt, and after long migrations ended up in England, and hence the similarity of the measurements in the two countries. Then, using measurements which were quite inaccurate, Smith created so-called facts such as: the length of the base (taken as 9,131 sacred cubits) divided by a sacred cubit, results in 365.24, i.e., the number of days in the year. Then by measuring the internal rooms of the Great Pyramid, a large amount of totally false data was created; for example, prophecies of the advent of the World Wars, and coming of the Messiah, and the end of the world.

A friend of his who shared his convictions, a certain Joseph Seiss, took up these ideas in his writings. The nature of Seiss' approach can be seen in his attitude to the book of Genesis in the Bible, and the Garden of Eden where the unfallen, pristine human beings lived. He harboured a belief that Adam was an historical person who may well have written part of the Bible himself. And since Adam grew up in the Garden of Eden, he would have a good idea as to its geography, and so this makes the geographical descriptions written in Genesis quite accurate. He wrote,

> Certainly no-one was so well qualified to write this book as Adam himself. And if he wrote anything, it must above all, have been this {book, Genesis}. Assuming that he, and not Moses, was the original narrator, we are greatly helped with regard to the {accuracy of the} references to the topography of Eden..." [17]

But just who taught Adam how to write in Hebrew, and ensure that his text was preserved until the time of the Hebrews, is left unsaid. There is no basis to these religious theories, nor to other claims such as the weight of the pyramid is one-thousand-billionth of the Earth's own weight. In fact, the actual weight of the monument can never be known for various reasons. For example, we don't know how many other

---

[17] Joseph A. Seiss, The great Pyramid; a miracle in stone; 1883, reprinted Steiner Books, N.Y. 1976.

chambers may be inside it, not yet discovered; one of which probably has the mummy of Khufu.

Other claims are made with respect to the over-all perimeter of the Great Pyramid, and how this can be used to discover the length of the year, etc. Now, at each corner of this four-sided monument square socket holes were made, and from these it is possible to calculate, **but only with limited accuracy,** the original proportions of the building. Only limited accuracy is possible, since the original casing stones have gone, and when this limitation is ignored, then more fanciful theories can be conjured up.

However, this building does have a number of significant mathematical proportions incorporated into its design, including very possibly, the number known as pi, which represents the ratio of the circumference of any circle to its diameter. Adding the length and the height of the King's Chamber, and dividing this by its width, does result in the value of pi. Furthermore, adding the length and the width of the sarcophagus in the King's Chamber, and dividing this by its height, also results in the value of the mathematical factor known as pi.

But one notes that if pi were known to the Egyptian pyramid builders, it was also known by other peoples of that era; even though apparently none of these people had the mathematical knowledge necessary to discover this. It seems to be incorporated in ancient Babylonian architecture, although it was not formally used as a specific value until the ancient Greeks. This fact again makes one consider whether some form of psychic intuiting was involved in the designing of such monuments. But it is also perhaps possible that it was an accidental discovery.

When we dismiss the many ungrounded ideas about the Great Pyramid and note the rational research done into its proportions, it could still be regarded as the most remarkable building and engineering feat on the Earth. This monument deserves a unique status for many reasons. One is the factor we have mentioned above – the extreme skill involved in its construction. We can note here that Khufu's father, Seneferu, had already built a pyramid about two thirds the size of Khufu's, but it was rather primitive in its construction, and lacked the many extraordinary features of the Great Pyramid. Likewise Khafre's pyramid is almost the same vast size as Khufu's, but much less technically perfect. But there are many other reasons to admire the Great Pyramid, let's see what the main points are, so that you can get the most from visiting it.

The extremely accurate astronomical alignment of the Great Pyramid

Mathematicians and astronomers have discovered over the past two hundred years some facts about the size and shape of this building which, though scientifically verified as true, appear to be not explainable, as they defy current understanding of what ancient cultures were capable of achieving. Indeed, to the more limited mainstream attitudes some facts about the Great Pyramid, (and we will not be considering irresponsible fantasies about the building), are only grudgingly admitted as being factual. Now this is an important point, because when you really take a good look at ancient sacred sites, at times they can present features which are beyond explanation; that is, beyond explanation to the worldview of modern times.

What are the extraordinary facts about the proportions of the Great Pyramid? Lets start with the some of the terrestrial features. Firstly, the ground on which the huge building was based, spread over 13 acres, was levelled to an accuracy of 1 in 1,000; this is an extraordinary feat, and appears to defy explanation. The idea that it is really just a simple procedure, requiring only that the site be flooded, and drained slowly, allowing the workmen to level off the prominent areas, as the water level receded, is quite wrong.

The renowned Egyptologist I.E.S. Edwards explained how remarkable it is that such an accuracy was achieved, because in the middle of the site, in what became the base level of the great pyramid, was a large central mound of solid rock which was never removed. He points out that this mound would have made it impossible for the builders to check visually the accuracy of the diagonal axes of the ground plan.[18]

Moreover, the Great Pyramid was also positioned so that its four sides face the four directions of the compass, i.e., its north side is almost exactly facing due north (only 3 minutes of arc from true north). Modern science has difficulties explaining how such an accuracy could be achieved, and applied to such a vast structure. The extreme accuracy of the alignment of the north and south sides can be explained away all too easily.

Some mainstream Egyptologists for example conclude that this was simply achieved by the ancients making some observation of the sun's position at sunrise and sunset and then marking these points, or by observing star movements, and again marking out these positions. And indeed such observations of the night sky were developed to a high level in earlier ages, for sea-faring and other purposes.

And Dr. Hawass has explained that his staff have found a series of round holes around the perimeters of the pyramid, parallel to the sides, and that these were probably used to hold stakes which held a string which gave the builders an accurate guide to the positioning of the stone blocks. He also tells us that trenches have been discovered which were for allowing water in, and later out, of the base area, and this enabled the level base of the site to be achieved. But this conclusion does seem to ignore the problem mentioned by Edwards, of the mound of rock in the centre of the pyramid's base.

But other scientists have concluded that with the Great Pyramid the degree of accuracy is so high that several subtle factors would distort the fine measurements needed, making such precise alignment impossible. These scientists in astronomy and meteorology have concluded that it is simply

---

[18] I.E.S. Edwards, The Pyramids of Egypt, George Rainbird Ltd, 1972.

not possible for a ground observer to set up the string so correctly on the stakes, as to find the north-south axis with the extreme degree of accuracy present in the Great Pyramid. This situation is discussed on the website of the long-established global scientific Society, Sigma Xi; (http://www.american scientist.org/).

These academics refer to really subtle factors distorting the actual true position of the sun making this impossible. These include the refraction of the sun's rays by the planet's atmosphere, and atmospheric pressure changes, and the fact the sun's precise position in the heavens alters in the course of a day (when it comes to making very precise measurements). It is not possible for any known system of observation, prior to GPS, to align this 13 acre monument with such precise accuracy. So, again we find an enigma with this awe-inspiring monument; perhaps a hint that other technologies or conscious states were involved, which to modern humanity are unknown?

The Great Pyramid is also sited on a precise dividing line of Egypt. Going north from the Giza plateau, one comes to the arc of the Nile delta. When a line is drawn back from the two sides of the delta to the Giza plateau, it forms a triangle. The location of the Great Pyramid on this plateau is at the very spot which forms the end point of this triangular shape; and thereby it is placed in the middle point of the Nile delta, in effect, in the centre of Egypt.

The remarkable optical accuracy of the casing stones & the equinox timing
Now, lets take a close look at another engineering feat achieved by the unknown supervisors of the building project, the casing stones. The Great Pyramid was originally encased with brilliant white limestone casing blocks, nearly all of which have gone. There were approximately 144,000 of them, and if laid out on the ground, they would cover 22 acres! Each was about 6ft (1.83m) thick and weighed about 15 tons. Each

one of these casing stones was fitted together so closely that the gap between them is only .020 of an inch (0.05cm). And, furthermore, the cement used to bind the stones together, is stronger than the stones, and is only 2/100th inch thick (0.06mm).

Now these stones were polished to brightly reflect the sunlight, and their mirror surface was ground very flat – to an accuracy of 1/100th inch (0.03cm). To really acknowledge what we are looking at here, we need to realize as Sir William Petrie pointed out, that this means the precision involved in this mirror-like casing of the vast building had an accuracy of .01 inch per 75 inches [19]; a precision which is acceptable to that of modern optometric lens-making. So the pyramid was covered in a seamless bright outer layer, that covered 22 acres.

These walls, whilst slightly cream-white in colour (as the Tura limestone discolours with age) being polished, would reflect the sun's rays quite well. Now, an intriguing fact was discovered by accident about these walls when a British military pilot in 1929 photographed the Great Pyramid from above. The four sides are actually slightly concave, or indented; there is a line running precisely up the middle of each side, making in effect each side into a two-sided wall. The play of light and shadow has made very visible the otherwise not perceptible indentation in the wall of the Great Pyramid. To see this photograph, check out http://www.world-mysteries.com./

This dividing of each wall means that the pyramid has, in effect, eight sides. And what this means is that, as Temple has shown, at sunrise and sunset as the rays of the sun were reflected off the eastern and western walls, respectively, the walls would then reflect the sunlight back.[20] However, amazingly, they would reflect the sunrise and the sunset for a

---

[19] = 0.025 cm to 190.5cm

[20] For technical ideas about the technique, see www.cheops-pyramide.ch/; for more about the reflecting power, see Robert Temple, The Crystal Sun, Arrow Books, 2000.

few days before the equinox and for a few days after the equinox – but not on the actual day of the autumn and spring equinox, then there would be no bright reflection. Because the midpoint of the walls, which faced exactly due west and due east, was actually a line, a slight crevice, where the walls joined! A vast mountain time-keeper, telling exactly when the crucial points in the solar cycle were approaching, or had gone.

And this awe-inspiring piece of engineering was created amongst peoples devoid of all but the most primitive of equipment. They apparently had no iron tools, not to mention laser-guided surveying equipment.[21] To find an answer as to why these ancient sacred places incorporate such extraordinary cosmic correspondences, we need to know something of the significance of cosmic energies to earlier peoples.

Furthermore, just as the dimensions of the Grand Gallery show the mathematical value of pi, so too do the over-all dimensions of the vast monument. The height of the pyramid appears to have been originally close to 146 metres, and the perimeter is close to 921 metres (exact measurements are not really possible), and if you divide the perimeter by twice the height the result is very close to (but not exactly) the famous Greek mathematical key figure of pi. But very significantly, these proportions also mean that the building is an exact model of the northern hemisphere, in harmony with the Earth's own perimeter, when measured at the equator, on a scale of 1: 43,200.

Now already these facts about the Great Pyramid are truly astonishing. A level of skill is involved that in part still defies explanation. And consequently the huge and complex project to build this miracle in stone is without parallel anywhere in the history of the world. So why did the builders go to so much trouble? A more pointed question would be, is the accepted explanation from Egyptologists correct, that this unique,

---

[21] Although there is evidence that a piece of iron bar was found inside the Great Pyramid, it remains a unique item in all of ancient Egypt, and hence any widespread use of iron tools is not a realistic idea.

extraordinary great and superbly complex engineering feat was undertaken only in order to build a tomb for a pharaoh? Or was it used for other purposes, purposes to do with the religious values of the ancient Egyptians?

Is there any evidence to show that this complex pyramid, (and indeed other pyramids) was constructed to serve the purpose of holding spiritual rites, to enable the priesthood to be in communion with their gods? In our next chapter we shall explore this theme. Until this question is clearly resolved, the nature of the Great Pyramid remains unclear. But already we have seen that, with its indented walls, it served as a time-keeper in regard to the equinox.

Chapter Four   The after-life in the religious belief system

Tombs and spiritual temples

It has naturally been assumed that the Great Pyramid, like other pyramids, was built as a burial chamber for the Pharaoh, during the Old Kingdom period, about 4,800 years ago. With regard to the Egyptian cult of the dead, and its architecture, some of the Egyptian burial chambers are indeed in the form of a pyramid, whilst many others are underground chambers. There are two interpretations of the Great Pyramid. The traditional one is that it is a burial chamber. The alternative view is that it was designed for that mysterious process, a core task of the priesthood, of encountering the divine realms.

However this alternative belief implies that within the religious life of the ancient Egyptians there was in existence for millennia, the Egyptian Mysteries, just as in ancient Greece. The Mysteries were institutions offering ritual procedures which were very secret and let the acolytes become initiated into the secrets of the spiritual worlds and its gods. These procedures, it is believed, enabled the acolyte to go up into spirit realms, and to learn from the gods. It also helped the priests to develop psychic capacities and to spiritualize themselves, pre-empting the spiritualizing process that the soul underwent in the after-life.

But what evidence is there that the ancient Egyptians ever had such a remarkable feature of their religious life? It is easy to adopt the mystical viewpoint, which has a thrilling feeling to it, but there is little point in marvelling at the Great Pyramid as a special place of esoteric activity, if in fact this is just an empty myth. So, what evidence is there for this belief? This pyramid is certainly within a mortuary site, with many associated burial monuments.

Why don't many mainstream Egyptologists believe that the Great Pyramid was anything more than a tomb? The first reason is that the ancient Egyptians themselves designated

Khufu's pyramid as a tomb, at least in a couple of documents. For example, in the Song of the Harper from the tomb of pharaoh Intef, itself a small mud-brick pyramid, these words occur,

> "…those who remain since the time of the ancestors, the gods (i.e., the deified kings) who existed long ago, who rest in their pyramids…" [22]

A similar situation occurs on the Sphinx-Stele von Amenhotep II (1448-1420 BC), the inscription here mentions how the pharaoh journeyed to Giza, and includes the words,

> "…he stayed a while there, walking his horse and the area and he gazed upon the wonderful resting-places of the pharaohs Cheops and Chephren, the Just." [23]

So reading this, one would naturally conclude that all the pyramids were tombs. Illustration 3 gives a clear view of the over-all structure of the Great Pyramid and its interior.

An excellent diagram is available on the internet showing the over-all Khufu complex, with its boat pits, satellite pyramids, solar boats and mortuary temple, see for example, www.onlineweblibrary.com. [24]

Actually the earliest notable tombs of the Egyptians were the mastaba, a simple elevated mud-brick platform. But with pharaoh Zoser in the 3rd dynasty the step pyramid was created, and inside this some partial mummified remains were discovered. Then the step pyramid was followed by the magnificent pyramids of the 4th dynasty (including those at Giza) which were naturally assumed to be tombs as well; especially since ancient Egyptian texts refer to them as tombs.

---

[22] Development of religion & thought in ancient Egypt, J. Breasted, p 182.
[23] See Frank Doernenburg's website: www. doernenburg.alien.de/alternativ
[24] The graphic itself originates, apparently, in the German site: www.semataui.de/AR/images - and if you know German, this is a very fine diagram as the buildings are named with tags.

Later in the New Kingdom tombs were made by excavating chambers underground; pyramids were no longer used.

However, one argument to support the idea that the Great Pyramid was not a tomb, is that no mummified remains were found in the pyramids at Giza. But a counter argument here is that some of the other pyramids were empty too. A mummy could have been inside a particular pyramid, but then removed by robbers or for re-burial elsewhere for safety; or destroyed if some political motivation was involved. And just to add another confusing factor, centuries later a mummy of another pharaoh or royal official could be placed inside a pyramid.

So what is the truth of this situation? It is clear that the pyramids were used as tombs, for pharaoh Intef did exactly that. But were any pyramids ever built for a mystical (initiatory) purpose? To answer this we need to consider **whether or not the ancient Egyptians ever had their own initiatory mysteries!** That is actually the only true beginning point of the argument. But first let's consider the after-life Mysteries of ancient Egypt.

The ancient Egyptians built magnificent tombs, and the after-life was a central focus of their entire existence; and ancient Egyptian burial chambers in the Valley of the Kings, with their illustrations of the rituals for the after-life, are profoundly interesting. They give a strong feeling that the priests had a clear knowledge of the mysterious journey of the dead as they leave the Earth and journey up to the realm of Ra. It is quite natural then for Egyptologists to consider Great Pyramid to be a huge tomb. If it is a tomb, then it belongs to the third aspect of the Giza Plateau, a Necropolis.

Giza Plateau Two: as a necropolis
The ancient Egyptians had a deep veneration for the sun god, and a deep-seated belief in the after-life. Indeed in ancient times all societies believed fully in the survival of the soul and its journey in the after-life, and the need to perform rituals for

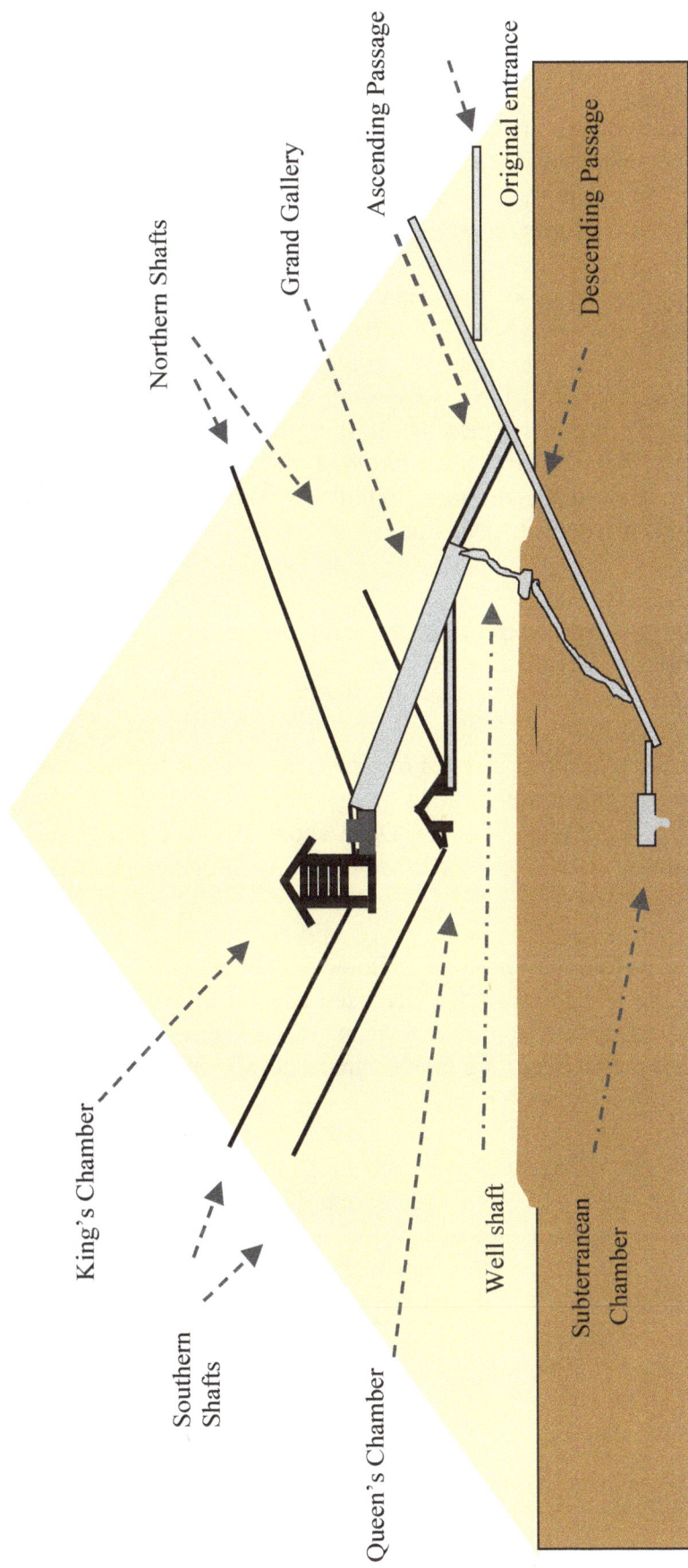

3 Khufu's Pyramid An outline of its unusual interior chambers and passages

Northern Shafts

Grand Gallery

Ascending Passage

Original entrance

Descending Passage

King's Chamber

Southern Shafts

Queen's Chamber

Well shaft

Subterranean Chamber

their ancestors. Some of the many tombs of prominent and royal persons elsewhere in ancient Egypt, especially in the Valley of the Kings, are truly breath-taking for their vast size, extending ever further and deeper underground.

The Egyptian Book of the Dead is perhaps the most detailed and most impressive book of instruction from ancient cultures, for carrying out the rituals to guide the souls of the dead. People also liked to have their tomb near to a sacred place, hence in Christendom, there is the siting of graveyards behind churches. And at Giza too, the wish to be near initiatory temples, and so the mortuary buildings of the pharaohs led thousands of people to seek burial there.

The complexity and depth of the after-life beliefs
Lets' briefly note the deeper statements about the after-life as found in ancient texts, to get some feeling for how this theme was viewed by the priesthoods. Firstly, the actual journey of the deceased is across a series of realms and past obstacles and opponents which are defined in a complex and profound manner – see the Book of the Dead about this. The result of this journey is that the deceased becomes transformed and merges with the deity.

Already in Chapter One of the Book of the Dead the priests entreat the god to allow the deceased soul to transform, and become immersed in the very being of the great sun god, Osiris. Some passages are extraordinary deeply mystical texts. For example Chapter 64 says,

> I am yesterday, today and tomorrow, and I have the power to be born a second time. I am the divine hidden soul who creates the gods, and who gives celestial meals unto the inhabitants of the Tuat (the Underworld), and Amentet and heaven.

And in chapter 77,

I, even I am the Khu (intelligence) who dwells with the divine Khu, whom the god Tem has created. The divine Khu who has come into being from the eyelashes of Tem (the Father-God).

So, the deceased has attained to a timeless state, and is feeling at one with a high divine-spiritual being, the creator of his or her own intelligence! A universal deity from whom all beings throughout the multi-level Creation gain their inner sustenance. But although in union with a lofty and sublime being, this passage tells that the soul also dimly discerns a still higher being, called Tem (or Atum), the great Creator of the gods themselves!

In another key text about the activity of the sun god during the night, which is the realm of the Dead, known as the Amduat, such deep statements as these are found,

The hidden road of Ament. The great god maketh his way over it in his holy boat, and he passeth over this road which has no water, and none to tow. He maketh his way by means of the words of power of Isis, and by means of the words of power of SEMSU (?), and the utterances of this great god himself; [these acting as] magical protectors, and he perform the slaughters of APEP in the Tuat, in this Circle, in his windings in the sky. Whosoever shall make [a copy of] these [pictures] according to the symbols, which are in writing at the northern side of the hidden palace in the Tuat. They shall act for him that maketh them as magical protectors in heaven and in earth. Whosoever knoweth them shall be as the Spirits, with Ra.

and again,

[This is] the hidden Circle of the Tuat (Underworld) through which this god maketh his journey so that he may come forth into the Eastern Horizon of the sky; it swalloweth eternally its images (or, forms) in the presence of the god REKH (?), who dwelleth in this City, and then it giveth them to those who are born and come into being in the earth. Whosoever shall make an exact copy of these forms according to the representations of the same at the eastern [portion] of the hidden Palace of the Tuat, and shall know it, shall be a spirit well equipped both in heaven and earth, unfailingly and regularly and eternally.[25]

An extraordinary text, indicating that the profound enigma of the after-life was deeply contemplated, and that they had a complex body of knowledge concerning mysterious correspondences between the terrestrial world and the spirit realms. So, is it really wise, is it really showing empathy for the cultural depth of the ancient Egyptian religion, to conclude that a priesthood who has created (or experienced) such lofty transcendent realities as these, actually had no over-arching Mysteries?

That is institutions that made possible specific knowledge of the after-life, as well as knowledge about attaining to higher consciousness, and perceiving how the gods brought forth creation, etc? Did the Egyptians really have no institutions providing rigorous spiritual procedures designed to raise the consciousness of the priest so he was able to enter into the realms of the Dead, and to accompany them on their journey?

One only has to consider that socially, the priest would be aware of just what is demanded of him or her, by the all-powerful pharaoh. The priesthood needed to develop an understanding of the dynamics that the deceased king expected that he will be encountering in these strange realms, where all cognition as we understand it, ceases. He needed to feel that the priests could offer real help to him in the after-life. The priests needed knowledge of realms where all sensory information ceases, and time and space are transcended. For

---

[25] see website; http://www.maat.sofiatopia.org/amduat.htm

this ability, Mysteries would be needed, not just formalized religious rites based on a rigid religious catechism.

Conservative senior Egyptologists, like Prof. Hornung, who don't have an intuitive viewpoint, have the view that the priesthood did not need any such Mysteries! Hornung acknowledges that many ancient Egyptian texts do refer to Mysteries, but he insists that they were only Mysteries in the sense of the formalized after-death duties of the priests. He writes,

> In Egypt, knowledge about the afterlife is not a secret teaching and is not part of initiation, revelation, or of a mystery cult, as in the later Greek tradition. It springs from a deep insight into the necessity for continuous regeneration, blocking the aging process of all being. (...) This means a continuous reconnection of the day-world and the night-world, of consciousness and the unconscious. [26]

In view of the depth and greatness of the after-life texts, this attitude seems rather inaccurate. In the understanding of ancient priesthoods, the journey of the acolyte during the initiatory process was similar to the journey of the soul in the after-life. The acolyte was able to ascend up the divine regions where the deceased soul went, on its journey up to the kingdom of Osiris (or Zeus, or Hu, etc).

This experience was viewed as very sacred, and not without its risks. Consequently it is scarcely likely that the priests officiating in the after-life rites would not be subject to some kind of spiritual training. Moreover, their experience of the sacred realms would result in a body of knowledge and insights that they would feel had to be kept secret from those not ready for exposure to such transcendent things. But what evidence is there of the ancient Egyptian priesthoods developing a body of initiatory knowledge?

---

[26] Erik Hornung and Theodor Abt, Knowledge for the Afterlife, 2003, Daimon Verlag, Germany, pp.144-145.

Chapter Five Did the ancient Egyptians have initiatory Mysteries?

Examining evidence for the Mysteries in ancient, pre-Hellenistic Egypt

A lot of ancient Egyptian texts exist which testify to exactly this situation, but they have not been correctly assessed in the past. However, a few intuitive scholars long ago, wrote learned articles pointing out the existence of real Mysteries in Egypt. In 1904 a German scholar Heinrich Schaefer, wrote about this presenting his convictions that indeed the ancient Egyptians did have secret Mysteries, like the Greeks. He presented some lines from a stele in Abydos created under pharaoh Sesostris III, written by I-cher-nofret, the vizier of Abydos. One of his titles was, "Keeper of the Secrets to the Word of God", which is very suggestive of an initiated person, perceiving the spiritual fiat of a deity. Schaefer translated the hieroglyphs into German,

> I carried out the service of a priest, the beloved son of Osiris … as leader of the House of Gold at the secrets of the Lords of Abydos…I adorned the god with his ornaments (crown, scepter, vestments, etc) in my capacity as Master over the Secrets. My service was that of one of the {--} priests. In adorning the god I was a person of pure arms, and I was a *Sm* priest with untainted fingers.[27]

It is clear from this passage that at Abydos there were secret spiritual processes and knowledge. And furthermore, that a high official of the Empire was entrusted with the task of supervising these. In recent years a number of Egyptologists have begun to write about their own research into these texts, and their new conclusions. They have written of their conviction that many of the numerous references to

---

[27] H. Schäfer, Die Mysterien des Osiris in Abydos unter König Sesostris II,Leipzig, J.C. Hinrichs'sche Buchhandlung 1904, pps.15-18.

"Mysteries" do actually refer to deep initiatory procedures and knowledge.

The evidence is very substantial. Egyptologists have noted for decades that passages in the literature for use in rituals of the after-life, were also used by the living, by priests. These passages are quite specifically intended to induce clairvoyant experiences of spirit beings. John Gee writes of this, mentioning the research of W. Federn, R. Merkelbach and quite a number of others.[28] Gee gives two texts from a hypostyle hall at Medinet-Habu,

> Let me initiate you and announce you into the horizon (i.e., sanctuary), so that you may see the lord of the Gods…let me initiate you into the great temple {of your father} Amun, lord of the gods.

This is quite clearly about the process of becoming a seer, and then becoming sanctified by receiving the blessing of the deity. And there are many more such inscriptions in great temples of Egypt, and even secret initiatory rooms.

Initiatory room hidden in a temple at Karnak
Karnak in southern Upper Egypt is a vast sacred site, it was called Ipet-isut in Egyptian, or Most Select of Places. As the main place for the worship of Amun it was developed and expanded over some 2,000 years. An unusual temple found in this complex, is understood by a new generation of Egyptologists to be an example of an initiatory site. It is a strange, secret room set in the huge temple precinct erected by Pharaoh Thothmes III, and known as the Botanical Garden. It is a small hall 15m (49ft) by 6m (20ft) decorated with flora and fauna. This room was secret; it was only accessible through a secret door placed about a metre above ground level,

---

[28] John Gee: Totenbuch-Forschungen: gesammelte Beiträge des international Totenbuch-Symposiums Sept 2005 edit. B. Backes, S.Stohr. p. 74-75 and also Prophets, initiation and the Egyptian temple JSSEA 31-2004.

in a wall in the ante-room. A series of statues is also there, arranged in two rows.

Researchers have noted that the plants and animals depicted here are in fact very unusual, including plants, animals and birds from Asia and East Africa. It is true that an inscription from Thothmes III here states that he has gathered these various things whilst on his military campaigns. But this does not really explain why they are depicted here, and in a secret room. Some academics have concluded that the depictions serve a purpose similar to several other monuments elsewhere in Egypt, namely that the strange flora and fauna, since they are not Egyptian animals, actually symbolize the wide and vast creative powers of Ra.

Another academic, Dimitri Laboury, has reached a definite conclusions about this Botanical Garden as part of the Egyptian Mysteries similar to those in western mystical groups, such as Freemasons, Theosophists, and students of Edgar Cayce. Laboury has concluded that this hidden chamber was an initiation chamber, a kind of holy of holies, set up for the use of the priests and Thothmes III. The Vizier in charge at Karnak, called Nespaqashuty, wrote a text in a similar style to that of the Vizier I-cher-nofret in Abydos, which was also engraved onto a stele. In this stele he makes also reference to being initiated in deep Mysteries, [29]

> I have seen Amun, in his *xxx*-sanctuary, in the hypostyle hall with statues, when he was emerging, like the rising sun, from the threshold between the divine and human worlds, and then I understood that the {various} gods are his emanations, as I saw them with him (arranged) in two rows, being myself secured in my garment with (the symbol of) Maat, thus I was, as

---

[29] Sacred Space and Sacred Functions, edit. F. Dorman & B Bryan, Studies in ancient oriental civilization, Vol 61, *Archaeological and textual evidence for the function of the 'botanical garden' of Karnak in the initiation ritual,* Dimitri Laboury FNRS Univ. of Liege Belgium //www.oi.uchicago.edu

the chief of the town (i.e., Vizier) like Thoth present at the court of Ra. [30]

What the high Vizier is speaking of here is a kind of seeing the divine, of witnessing a deity becoming perceptible in the secret initiation chamber hidden in the huge Karnak complex! And furthermore, the Vizier reports that he perceived (obviously in a vision) that the various ranks of spiritual beings are themselves the creation of the great sun spirit. This is obviously undeniable evidence of the belief in and existence of, initiatory Mysteries.

A new attitude from younger Egyptologists
Further evidence for the existence of secret spiritual knowledge can be found in all sorts of places. For example, there is an indication of this in an ancient text known as the Carlsberg 1 Papyrus. It is a commentary on the Book of Nut which deals with the mysterious realms of the after-life. This book was written on the walls in the Cenotaph of pharaoh Seti 1 (or Sethos 1) at Abydos, and dates from ca.1,300 BC.

The commentary, written later on in the Hellenistic Age, deliberately placed 'blinds' or false letters in its explanations of the book, so that the uninitiated, reading this text, would not discover certain secrets of these realms.[31] In 2002 a German book was published, Ägyptische Mysterien ('Egyptian Mysteries'), with 10 essays from various Egyptologists who presented evidence for their growing conviction that the ancient Egyptians did indeed have initiatory mysteries. [32]

An even more lofty experience of the kind was reported by the Vizier of Abydos, was testified to by the pharaoh Thothmes III himself, as recorded on another stele,

---

[30] I have slightly altered the translation for readability.
[31] Prof. Otto Neugebauer, writing in the Journal of Near Eastern Studies, 4,1-38, 1945, p. 26.
[32] Jan Assmann / M.Bommas, edits, Ägyptische Mysterien? W. Fink Verlag, Munich.

I stood in the northern colonnaded hall
as Amun appeared out of the holiness of his realm
His beauty made heaven and earth festive
and began great wonders, for his radiance
in the eyes of the high priests was like that of the dawn.
The serving priests gave praise to him, …
For me he opened the portals of heaven,
he opened the door of his sanctuary.   *[33]
I flew up to heaven like a divine falcon
and beheld his secret image in heaven.
I prayed to his majesty…
I saw the forms of his realms   *
on his secret pathways to heaven.[34]

Here we see quite clearly the proof that the ancient Egyptians indeed had their Mysteries, and that they were of an initiatory kind. Even if one dismisses this entire text as a politically motivated pretence, it still remains proof that in this culture the process of being initiated was a known reality.

This has the really significant implication that the ancient Egyptians built many great temples and monuments to serve their spiritual Mysteries. A new era of deeper, more correct understanding of the ancient Egyptian culture is now being allowed to emerge, as the younger Egyptologists allow a more insightful view of the Egyptian culture to emerge.

Many buildings of ancient Egypt now have to be viewed as designed to facilitate the secretive process of training priests to gain higher consciousness, and commune with their gods. So now it becomes both sensible and valid to conclude that some of the monuments, including some pyramids, were Mystery

---

[33] The Egyptian hieroglyph here '*pr*' is often better translated not as 'horizon', but in its other meanings. Here especially, it means 'sanctuary' and then 'realms'.
[34] Original text translated in *Urkunden der 18. Dynastie Erster Band*, edit. K.Sethe, Leipzig, J. Hinrichs'sche Buchhandlung 1906; German version in Jan Assmann / M.Bommas, edits, *Ägyptische Mysterien?* W. Fink Verlag, Munich 2002.

temples, and not, or not exclusively tombs, nor mortuary temples. And this could include all three major pyramids on the Giza Plateau.

The pyramid of Khafre (Chephren)
The impulse behind the initiative for a spiritual site as distinct from a burial site was not limited to the achievement of the pyramid of Khufu; for the neighbouring huge pyramid of pharaoh Khafre also shows some intriguing features in its passages and rooms, as Egyptologist I. E. S. Edwards comments. These features are in fact similar to those in the Great Pyramid, although on a much simpler scale. It has two so-called burial chambers, one of them is described as abandoned.

And the final burial chamber actually has small replicas of the mysterious shafts found in the Great Pyramid! These have been cut into the walls, about one foot (0.3m) in length, and in addition, it has an inexplicable sloping passageway which connects the lower and the higher chambers. It seems that although Khafre's pyramid is an inferior copy of the Great Pyramid, it was also intended for spiritual rites.

The pyramid of Khafre is an attempt to replicate the Great Pyramid, but in circumstances which lacked access to the same level of expertise. Indeed the remarkable accuracy of alignments and precision construction of the Great Pyramid are entirely lacking here. In Khafre's pyramid, the limestone blocks are just placed next to each other, often without any mortar, often leaving substantial gaps between stones, and the precision of the joints and of entire courses of blocks is often very poor.[35]

Since Khafre was the son of Khufu, the original architectural genius and his skilled assistants responsible for the Great Pyramid, would have died sometime before, and his successors were simply not able to replicate his achievements. Since

---

[35] See http://touregypt.net/featurestories/ for more on this

Khufu's pyramid was built for primarily religious ritual purposes, rather than a tomb, it is likely that Khafre's pyramid, which imitates the Great Pyramid, was also built for these same purposes. There are several reasons for coming to this conclusion.

The pyramid of Khafre has passages and chambers which seem to be similar to that of Khufu, (although of a much simpler nature). There is a lower chamber, and an upper one, giving the impression at first that, as with Khufu's pyramid, the lower one was abandoned. However just as in Khufu's pyramid there was no abandonment of a chamber, but specific symbolic and pragmatic purpose behind these chambers, a similar situation seems to be the case with Khafre's pyramid.

As the Egyptologist Edwards comments, there are some odd features to the internal design of Khafre's pyramid, which are nearly impossible to explain. There are firstly, rectangular cavities cut into the walls, as if to replicate the mysterious shafts of Khufu's pyramid, but they only went in 12 inches, see website: www.guardians.net for illustrations of this. But the more striking enigma concerns the two tunnels entering this pyramid. Some distance along the lower tunnel, a chamber was cut out on its eastern side; this is defined as a burial chamber. But then the other, higher tunnel was cut down into the pyramid, and this terminates eventually in another chamber, higher up inside the building, (and this is also defined as a tomb).

This is defined as the result of a mistake, or an unforeseen problem with the logistics of constructing this huge monument. However the mystery deepens when we see how the builders constructed an ascending passageway from the lower tunnel that goes up and merges with the higher shaft. To join up the two tunnels is quite illogical, architecturally, if the chambers were tombs; one just would not do this. But this conjoining is similar to the conjoining of tunnels, and hence the chambers, inside the Great Pyramid.

And with Khafre's pyramid, archaeological research has discovered that its lower temple at the end of the causeway, adjacent to the waterways that lead off from the Nile, has **two** ramps going down to the water-way. Only one causeway is needed for a royal funeral procession, whereas two could play a role in symbolic rites of the priesthood. And furthermore, as regards the Valley Temple of Khafre, there are no signs of it ever being a mortuary building, a place where the body was mummified. As Dr. Hawass comments, the ground plan, wall reliefs, cult objects etc, do not show any association with the process of mummification and funerary needs. This was probably true of Khufu's valley temple too, but only parts of that have been found under layers of soil, during civic engineering projects.

The upper mortuary temple and the lower mortuary temple in the valley near the Nile, are both designed for religious use, but neither of them proves that Khafre was entombed in the second pyramid. The valley temple had many statues of Khafre inside it, and this indicates that the after-life rituals of the pharaoh were carried out there. There is a sarcophagus in one of the chambers of his pyramid, but it was empty, similar to Khufu's pyramid, and Khafre's mummy has never been found. If the pyramid was used for religious rites and not as a tomb, then it is quite possible that Khafre made a decision similar to Khufu, to be interred near to his pyramid, rather than inside it.

The Pyramid of Menkaure or Mykerinos is also significant here, because inside this pyramid, built by the grandson of Khufu, there are many features that seem to be irrelevant for a tomb. Again see website: www.guardians.net for excellent 3D graphics of this strange interior. Inside there is another lidless sarcophagus; a sign of a ritual purpose rather than a burial (see next section). And there is a multi-compartment chamber and various other rooms and passages that are not necessary for a tomb.

Khafre's Valley Temple

Khafre's Valley Temple is at the end of the causeway from the Khafre's pyramid. It is obviously therefore integrated into the scheme of Khafre's pyramid and its causeway, and is therefore also from the Old Kingdom era. It is constructed of huge blocks of granite which were brought by boat down the Nile from Aswan some 450 miles (725kms) away. It once had two causeways from its eastern side going down to the Nile; these terminated at the temple in two large wooden doors, one of which was dedicated to Bastet, the other to Hathor.

Inside it still shows emplacements made for four very large sphinxes, 8m in length (26 ft), two at each entrance, (although they are small compared to the great sphinx, which is nearly ten times longer). This fact of four other leonine sphinxes being carved for this temple of Khafre affirms again that the sphinx dates from the Old Kingdom, and that extensive religious rites were performed in this temple, in veneration of the sun god. Inside this monument, in a great hall, about 10 statues of Khafre were found, and fragments of others indicate that there were once 23 or 24 of these.[36]

A tomb and an initiatory temple
As we noted earlier, there are many people in mystical circles in the western world, who believe that the Great Pyramid belongs to what we call the second aspect of the Giza Plateau: a religious-spiritual site. A site designed to facilitate initiatory processes. Yet mainstream Egyptologists have always maintained that the Great Pyramid was built to serve as a tomb, and we have looked at some historical documents showing that indeed it was regarded as a tomb. But, as we shall now see, there are some substantial arguments in favour of it being an initiatory place.

A confusing statement? Yes, but the solution here is simple; the pyramid of Khufu and Khafre (and Menkaure as well) **are tombs for their pharaohs but, they were also initiation temples**. The mummy of each of these pharaohs was not

---

[36] www.guardians.net/Hawass/mortuary1

necessarily placed inside, at least not in the chambers that we have so far discovered. The chambers were designed for initiation rituals, not for burials. But these two pyramids are still the resting place of the pharaoh; the mummy would have been hidden in a chamber somewhere else inside these huge, mountainous buildings.

It is time to get clear about what kind of monuments were built on the Giza Plateau. There are ritual temples and small pyramids, boat pits, satellite temples and a family temple, for the relatives of Khufu. Here all three of the main pyramids are found in this scheme, for both Khafre and Menkaure had pyramids built that have interior spaces which indicate complex purpose, a purpose beyond that of a grave.

However, both pyramids were probably used as a tomb as well; the mummy of the pharaoh being placed in some other room, away from the initiation chambers. So, an empty sarcophagus is not conclusive evidence that a particular pyramid was never a tomb; the mummy could be lying somewhere else in the pyramid. And later on, an initiation chamber could be used as a tomb by a member of the royal family, once the original purpose of the chamber was forgotten or ignored.

The Great Pyramid was certainly sited in a large necropolis complex, including temples for the after-life rituals, and also many tombs for high officials of the court, etc. You can see in our illustrations, the mortuary temple and the causeway down to the Nile, and the smaller pyramids for his family members, and pits for storing the solar-boat which would take the deceased up into heaven, etc.

The term mortuary temple means a temple where the mummy would be prepared, or if prepared elsewhere, from whence it was taken during a ritual process into its tomb. But as Dr. Zahi Hawass points out, the doors on these temples in the valley near the Nile, are too narrow to allow for the funeral procession to proceed through, on its way into the Great Pyramid, or the pyramid of Khafre and Menkaure.

Each of the three main pyramids has a causeway, a substantial avenue of stone in parts beautifully decorated, reaching down to waterways coming off the Nile River. In illustration 4 these three causeways are clearly depicted, leading off from the pyramids; the one from Khufu's pyramid is only vaguely visible today, as the waterways have long ago disappeared, swallowed up by encroaching suburbs of Cairo. Through these waterways, funeral boats and barges carrying construction material for temples and tombs were able to moor near to the Giza plateau.

The mummy would be brought by funeral barge along the Nile, and then up to a causeway, and onto the plateau. But we have no actual proof that a mummy of Khufu or Khafre was ever brought up and placed in the pyramids named after them.

Boats carrying officials and priests involved in spiritual rituals at the Great Pyramid, and Khafre's pyramid and in the Sphinx temples, would also need such causeways up onto the plateau. Over several centuries many tombs were cut out of the rock here, to house the bodies of deceased officials and royalty. A similar arrangement of accommodating the activity of a necropolis and also the rituals carried out to help the living, was designed at the sacred sites on the Salisbury Plains of England, such as Stonehenge and Durrington Walls. Illustration 4 identifies in mauve color the tombs and temples, etc, that were built there for helping the deceased in the after-life. Illustration 5 identifies in blue color the buildings and monuments that make the Giza Plateau a site for spiritual rituals and worship of deities.

The point here is that, as we noted earlier, to the ancients the initiatory quest takes the soul into the same realms as those we enter after death, and so when the pharaoh did die, he would want to be buried somewhere near, or in, such a special pyramid. Indeed there is a very old legend which says that

4 THE GIZA PLATEAU: Aspect 2: a site for initiatory rituals and worship of deities

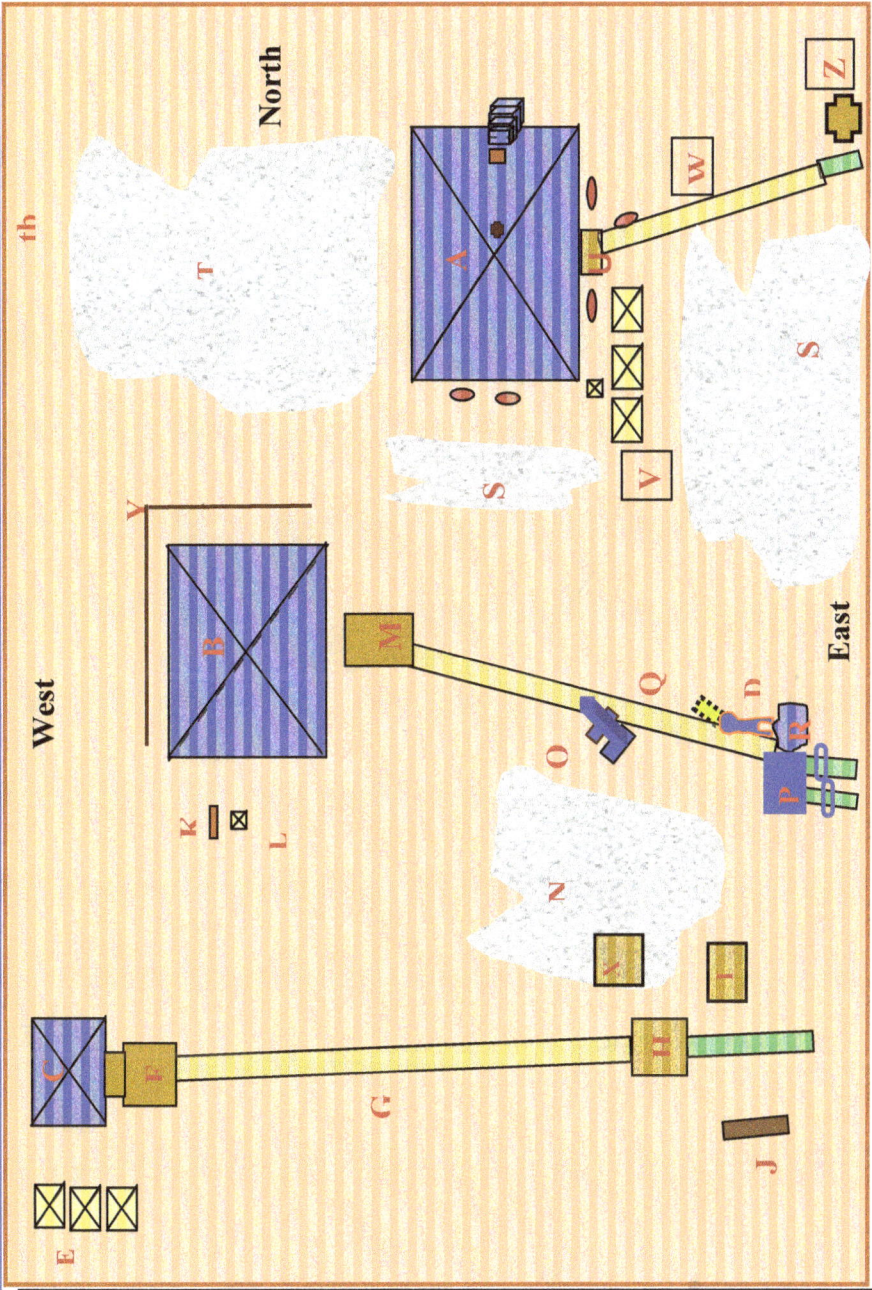

North

West

East

th

A Pyramid of Khufu / Cheops
B Pyramid of Khafre (Chephren)
C Pyramid of Menkaure (Mykineros)
D Great Sphinx
E Menkaure family pyramids
F Menkaure ritual Temple
G Menkaure Causeway
H Menkaure's valley temple
I Necropolis priests' houses
J Wall of the Crow
K Khafre serdab (ba tomb)
L Khafre family pyramid
M Khafre ritual temple
N Central Mastaba (tombs) area
O Underground Osiris chamber
P Khafre Valley Temple
Q Khafre Causeway
R Sphinx Temple
S Eastern Mastaba area
T Western Mastaba area
U Khufu ritual temple
V Khufu family pyramids
W Khufu Causeway (traces left)
X tomb of Khentkawes
Y Khafre quarry perimeter
Z Khufu Valley Temple (destroyed)
tb = tomb of the birds

Khufu solar boat pits
Khafre solar boat pits
ramps to water-ways (destroyed)
dead-end tunnel from sphinx
entry ramp Grt. Pyramid (assumed)
Gash in upper wall of Pyramid
hidden swivel-door entrance
hidden swivel-door entrance

67

5   THE GIZA PLATEAU: Aspect 3: a necropolis where rituals for pharaohs and others were held

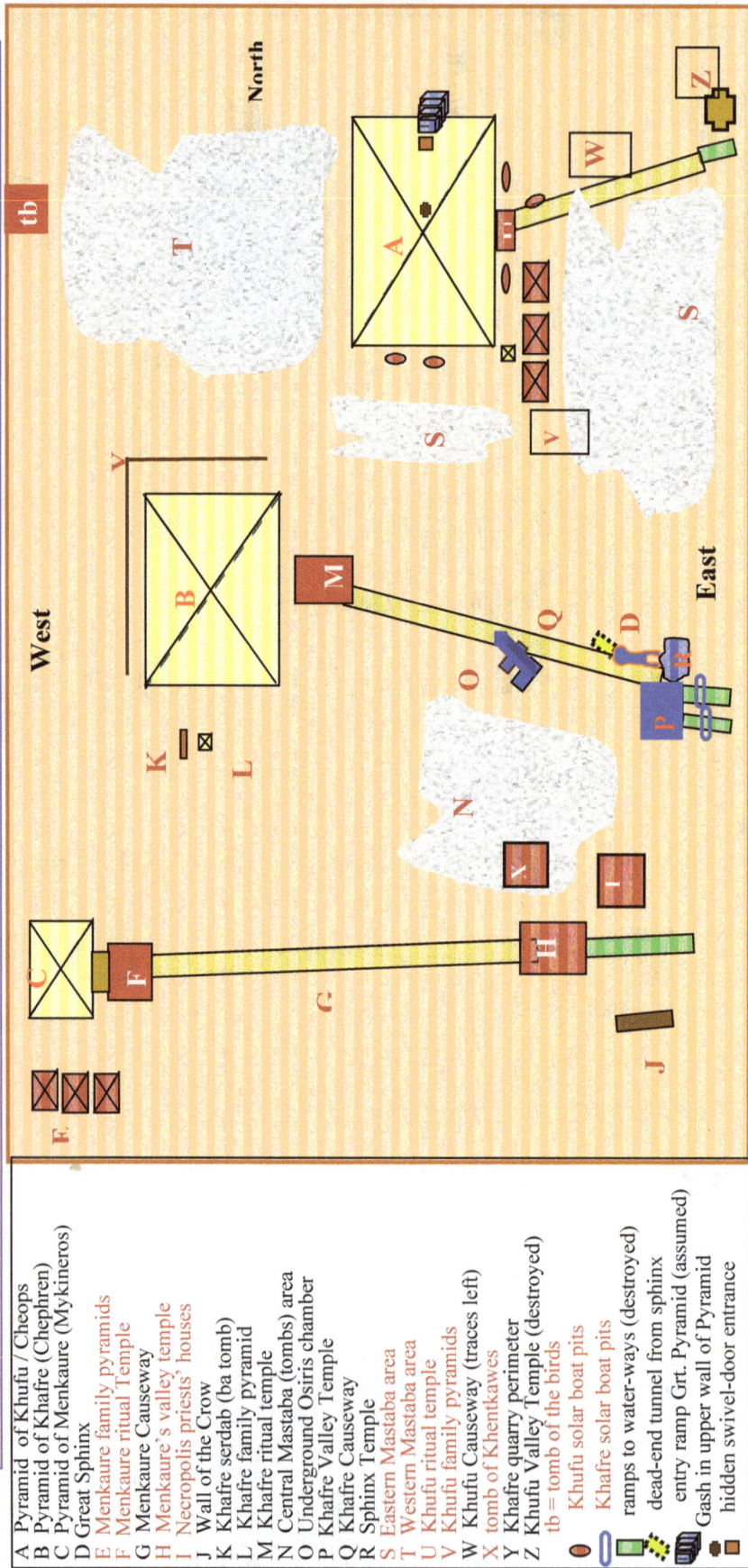

North

West

East

A Pyramid of Khufu / Cheops
B Pyramid of Khafre (Chephren)
C Pyramid of Menkaure (Mykineros)
D Great Sphinx
E Menkaure family pyramids
F Menkaure ritual Temple
G Menkaure Causeway
H Menkaure's valley temple
I Necropolis priests' houses
J Wall of the Crow
K Khafre serdab (ba tomb)
L Khafre family pyramid
M Khafre ritual temple
N Central Mastaba (tombs) area
O Underground Osiris chamber
P Khafre Valley Temple
Q Khafre Causeway
R Sphinx Temple
S Eastern Mastaba area
T Western Mastaba area
U Khufu ritual temple
V Khufu family pyramids
W Khufu Causeway (traces left)
X tomb of Khentkawes
Y Khafre quarry perimeter
Z Khufu Valley Temple (destroyed)
tb = tomb of the birds

Khufu solar boat pits
Khafre solar boat pits
ramps to water-ways (destroyed)
dead-end tunnel from sphinx
entry ramp Grt. Pyramid (assumed)
Gash in upper wall of Pyramid
hidden swivel-door entrance

68

Khufu is buried somewhere near, perhaps even underneath, the Great Pyramid. It is also understandable that in the course of time many of the ancient Egyptians wanted their final resting place to be near the three pyramids on the Giza plateau. But all this does not have to mean that the Great Pyramid itself was constructed solely as a burial place. There is no contradiction in it being used primarily as a spiritual site, and also being in an area which was the focal point of burial chambers of privileged people.

The underground Osiris Chamber

The underground Osiris Chamber is also shown in our illustrations. This feature consists of a series of underground chambers cut down underneath the ground, in a zig-zag pattern near to Khafre's Causeway. It was made about 1,550 BC and was used no doubt for spiritual rites connected with the primary motif in ancient Egyptian myths; the death and resurrection of Osiris. This drama of the death and re-birth of Osiris from his sarcophagus is however, the prototype for the initiation experience of the acolyte in the Mysteries. It may also have been intertwined with the Egyptian creation scene, where the power of the sun god brings forth new life out of the waters of chaos (called Nut).[37] At the bottom of the shaft in the Osiris Chamber was the special chamber where a sarcophagus was found, placed on an elevated mound of earth, surrounded by a small water channel. This is probably the famous tomb of Osiris mentioned by the Greek historian, Herodotus in the 5th century BC.

The sarcophagus is sunk down into the rock, and has four pillars in the rectangular chamber. It is similar to the spiritual Osireion at Abydos where another such sarcophagus was once installed, and surrounded by a water channel. All of this was placed inside in a rectangular shaped chamber with five pillars; a strong indication of a space designed for ritual purpose. Now we shall consider the Great Pyramid as a monument for spiritual rituals, in more detail.

---

[37] For an excellent 3D diagram of the underground chamber see, www.archaeology.org/0009.

Chapter Six The Great Pyramid as a temple for religious rites

The purpose of the Great Pyramid

An examination of the interior of the Great Pyramid suggests strongly that it, like the pyramid of Khafre and Mycineros, was designed to enable people to become initiated. That is, in the understanding of the ancient priesthood of Heliopolis, the acolyte would be able to experience for themselves the realms of Osiris. All three pyramids were probably also used in some way as tombs as well. So both the outer appearance, and the interior spaces of such a monument **may well look like a tomb.** For the realms of the spirit where the ancient mystics believed they journeyed in their sacred rites, are the same realms where the souls of the dead went, as described in the Egyptian Book of the Dead.

The spiritual rites were considered a sacred process in ancient times, because the Egyptian acolyte understood that he could pre-empt the difficult experiences undergone in the after-life journey by attaining to a high spiritual state. And thereby after his own death he could arrive safely at the blessed realm of Osiris. It was believed that the acolyte could know about the journey into spiritual realms, which is undertaken by the dead in the natural course of existence. The pharaoh could well decide to make such a temple into his tomb, but not right in the special chambers. All these factors blur the evidence for its true purpose, to later archaeologists.

Now this means that there is a link between the purpose of a burial chamber and an initiation chamber, and hence they may share similar architectural features. This creates a significant architectural interpretation challenge, and we meet this in regard to the old Celtic or Megalithic practise of burying their dead in a rock barrow or cairn, of a similar type to that used for spiritual rituals. It is important to note here that the Egyptians did construct pyramid shaped tombs, starting with a pyramidal tomb at Meidum that had been built as a seven-tiered monument, and which was later converted into a normal, smooth-walled pyramid. So, it is natural that those Egyptologists, who are not open to the idea of spiritual training for the Egyptian priesthoods, would think of the Great Pyramid as exclusively a tomb.

We note that such an extraordinary building as the pyramid of Khufu exceeds the purposes of a tomb, even for a Pharaoh, by a very significant margin, in terms of its complexity. As we noted above, although this chamber is furnished with a lidless sarcophagus, it was in fact devoid of any mummy when for the first time ever, in 832 AD, intruders entered the chamber. Some people have concluded on very slim evidence that it was burgled just a century or two after it was built; and that the mummy was stolen then.

But this is extremely unlikely since in all probability this pyramid was in active use as the greatest sacred site in the land. And moreover, there is no evidence of any forced entry, intruders, or urgent departure. And since the entrance to the corridor which leads up to the Chamber had been sealed off with large granite plugs, no-one had gained access by using the right entry, the swivel door up on the north wall, since it was sealed.

No-one that is, until the invading workmen forced their way inside, in the ninth century, by going around the plugs. But some people nevertheless speculate that intruders may have bored their way through the vast wall from deep underground, and entered the chambers by way of the Well Shaft, and taken the gold treasures as well as the mummy. But this scenario is most unlikely; it is too narrow an approach to take, it overlooks the various features of the great building. Just consider the idea realistically.

The robbers would enter in, but just how they could get entry and then force their way into the bottom of this huge monument, and then proceed up through it, to access the well shaft, which leads up to the so-called burial chamber, is left unsaid. There is no evidence of any tunnel that gives access to the well shaft. How did they then manage to back-fill the tunnels they made from some other point of forced entry, and clamber up and down the dangerous well-shaft, rummage through the chambers, and yet evade all later detection by modern researchers? This is all left unanswered.

But anyway, they decide to take not just the jewels and gold from the mummy, but also decide to lug the mummy itself down the dangerous, narrow Well Shaft; for the sarcophagus is empty, the mummy of the pharaoh has never been found. However, even unburdened by an eerie, worthless mummy, a descent down this narrow shaft is a really dangerous task. And then our intrepid robbers decide to also drag the utterly worthless, half-ton granite lid of the sarcophagus down the shaft as well!

But here the lack of objectivity of this mainstream conclusion shows itself, for in fact this lid is too wide to fit down the shaft. It simply cannot go down it, and since no fragments of it remain, one is left with the most unlikely scenario that the robbers decided to break it into pieces and to then very carefully sweep up all the tiny bits left over.

The conclusion is obvious; the sarcophagus was never a coffin, but instead was used for spiritual rites. There are indeed small holes on the top surface of the sarcophagus, and these are precisely what would be used to anchor a lid. But it is entirely reasonable to conclude they are there to fully complete the symbolism of the rite! Inside the Great Pyramid are a number of chambers which are very strange in their design and structure. These chambers have acquired inappropriate names, and their inherently odd structure is not a focus of mainstream research.

Strange internal chambers & passageways
From the diagram in illustration 3 we saw that the Great Pyramid has a series of chambers and passageways, more complex than the internal chambers of the other two pyramids

on the Giza plateau. Entering the pyramid by getting access to an opening situated about 100ft up on the north wall, one could then venture down the Descending Passage until it peters out. One finds oneself in a roughly finished cavity, deep in the gloomy and stifling depths of the huge monument. Leading off from here is another short passageway that ends abruptly; below your feet is a dead-end pit. But earlier on, if you had left the Descending Passage and proceeded up along the Ascending Passage, then this pathway would lead you to a corbelled gallery. This is a room of large proportions, called the "Grand Gallery", whose walls taper towards each other in seven stages, thus making the upper area progressively smaller, see illustration 6.

Now inside the Gallery, if you continue on straight ahead, you enter a tunnel that terminates in the smallish "Queen's Chamber" (so named by the Arab intruders in the 9th century, as it had a few features similar to the burial chamber for an Arabian Queen). But actually, if one had stayed in the Grand Gallery, you could climb up a small wall and onto a narrow path leading upwards, right through the Grand Gallery, and eventually one reaches the room called the King's Chamber.

This upper chamber is accessed at the end of the Grand Gallery by heaving yourself up over a very high step, and then walking on through a number of narrowed spaces, including a small space which requires you to bend right over and clamber along a metre or so, before entering the central chamber, where is found the sarcophagus, empty and lidless. (Today a wooden ramp removes the need to clamber up the last very high step; a stone block which is very worn down, indicating millennia of use.)

The usual interpretation of these internal structures is that they all arose from the efforts of the builders to create a suitable tomb for the pharaoh Khufu. The lowest, roughly finished subterranean chamber was built first of all they say, and then it was regarded as a mistake. That is, the builders decided to abandon this part of the huge pyramid and make a new chamber for the mummy much higher up. So they then constructed the Queen's Chamber, but that also was abandoned as not good enough (a second mistake amidst the construction of such a masterpiece!), and finally the uppermost chamber, the King's Chamber, was built. We shall examine this theory of multiple mistakes in the world's most brilliant engineering achievement, later.

Above its ceiling the King's Chamber has five mysterious small compartments made of huge granite slabs, and it also has narrow vents which go to the outer layer of the pyramid. In recent times, various New Age writers have stated that these shafts were all aligned to several important stars at the same date long ago in the past; as we shall see, this is incorrect. However, these shafts could be explained as relating to the after-death journey of the deceased pharaoh. And yet they are also accurately interpreted as relating to an initiation process of some kind.

There is another very curious feature to the pyramid in regard to apparently missing items. At the entrance to the upper chamber (the King's Chamber) there are several small compartments which you have to squeeze through, before entering the chamber itself, with its sarcophagus. These compartments appear to have a portcullis arrangement. That is, the walls have wide channels in them which could allow several slabs of rock to be lowered down from the ceiling, and reach the floor, sealing them off, and thus blocking access to the King's Chamber. But no such three slabs of rock were ever found inside the Great Pyramid.

The rather narrow explanation actually goes so far as to say that these were stolen too (!), some centuries before the Arabian workers forced their way into the monument. So, again intrepid thieves crept into the vast building, through a secret pathway, and made off with three worthless pieces of heavy stone (and the worthless sarcophagus lid), without damaging the surrounding panels at all. There must have been easier ways to

6 Procession to the King's Chamber . A cut-away view of the Grand Gallery. Right: the Asc. Passage to the Grand Gallery. Yellow triangular area on the right: has the wall cut fully away, showing the access tunnel to Queen's Chamber, and overhead, in red-brown, the start of the Grand Gallery's elevated walkway. Copyright the author.

7 **The King's Chamber** with its solid granite coffer (damaged by souvenir hunters) in the bare granite chamber. A tomb or an initiation chamber?

get some slabs of stone in ancient Egypt! The granite sarcophagus is shown in illustration 7. An intuitive observer can see that it is much more probable that, just as there was never a lid to the sarcophagus, the portcullis too, was symbolic – there were never any such slabs of rock at the entrance to the King's Chamber. It is much more likely that the mysterious internal rooms and passages are symbolic, are a sacred landscape, with a message.

In fact when the Great Pyramid was explored for the first time in the 19th century, the air in that shaft was extremely stifling, due to the presence of bats and small rodents which had died. At least one of the first surveyors in the 19th century to venture into it lost consciousness and had to be carried up out of it. So, any thieves trying to escape via the narrow, dangerous well, especially if hauling heavy granite rock slabs, would have probably collapsed in the effort.

However there is also speculation that the well shaft may have been cut down into the lower part of this great monument somewhat later than the rest of the chambers. The shaft is irregular and erratic in its descent through the masonry, and consists in part of irregularly shaped blocks. This is considered as evidence for a later date of construction, because, so goes the argument, the original builders would not work in such a crude way, cutting through their own masonry work. But this is highly unlikely, if the building has an architectural message. Then the roughness of the walls here is a deliberate symbolism, as we shall see later when we consider again the sacral landscape of these chambers.

There are no reports after 500 BC from travellers to Egypt revealing any knowledge of how to enter the Great Pyramid from the original hinged doorway. So we conclude that sometime before this date, the priesthood in charge of this awesome building ordered that its Ascending Passage be blocked by the three granite plugs that had been stored in the Grand Gallery. The outer wall's swivel door was then closed very carefully to camouflage it, and the huge monument remained inaccessible for many centuries, until entry into it was gained by force in the 9th century.

Reading the language of the strange chambers

Now we can look at the alternative view, namely that this complex internal structure reveals that the Great Pyramid was designed for another purpose. This view says that the supposed mummy was never there, that Khufu is buried elsewhere in the huge pyramid. This attitude is affirmed by several features of the great Pyramid. For example, the fact noted earlier that the sarcophagus although given the little indentations along one edge needed to secure a lid, never actually had a lid.

But very importantly, this sarcophagus in the King's Chamber is too wide to be pulled up through the Ascending Passage towards the Grand Gallery; it cannot be towed up this corridor.[38] So, for the sarcophagus to be placed there, it must have been put in the Chamber whilst the pyramid **was still being built**. But, this would mean that, if this was a burial place, then the pharaoh, once he had died, would have had to be carried up through all the passages, as a solitary, unprotected mummy and then finally placed in his intended, but permanently unlidded, unsealed sarcophagus; a most unlikely proposition!

The sarcophagus would have to be sealed to protect the body of Khufu from vermin, especially as mummification was a new practise, begun in this era, or shortly before. All this gives the impression that the building was not intended to be simply a tomb for a pharaoh. Lets get some background to all this, which is relevant to all the sacred sites which we shall discuss.

Just before we finish our discussion of the traditional view about the use of these internal chambers, we saw earlier that the Descending Passage is amazingly accurate in its engineering. Now, if the non-holistic attitude were right, and the subterranean chamber was the first choice for a tomb for

---

[38] And it would have to be awkwardly, indeed disrespectfully, turned on its side to fit through the antechamber of the King's Chamber

the Pharaoh, the question arises, why would the builders construct it to such awe-inspiring perfection, **when it was still only in its preliminary stage**, and then later abandon it, in favour of a higher chamber?

In other words, although it was cut out to an almost incredible standard of technical perfection it was, in the mainstream theory, actually just the rough preliminary tunnel, It was waiting to be greatly widened, to form a passageway big enough to allow the royal mummy in its big sarcophagus to be transported down, together with furniture, etc., for the pharaoh's after-life.

This is a false argument; the passageway was obviously finished off to perfection, it was complete as it was; see illustration 8. It had not been built as the preliminary form of a wider funeral passageway. Its purpose emerges as we examine holistically the structure of the Great Pyramid. This non-insightful theory, possibly starting with the Egyptologist Cottrell, needs to be put to rest. The passage has to do with enabling an acolyte to observe a star from the miserable pit deep down inside the monument, as part of some unknown religious rite.

To examine the alternative view of this great monument, which considers it to have a spiritual function, we need to look at the diagram of the Great Pyramid (illustration 9), so we can start to discover the meaning of its internal rooms and passages. Firstly, see how the entrance passage comes to a junction, a parting of the ways, where one path leads upwards, and another leads down and becomes the Descending Passage. If we go down this passage, then we go down to a subterranean pit, with a few false exits; so we come to a miserable dead-end.

Whereas if one took the Ascending Passage, then one would eventually come to an opening, and ahead lies the entry to another tunnel, which eventually leads to a much more pleasant chamber, the so-called Queen's Chamber. The Queen's Chamber in its structure has much more positive and interesting features. This chamber actually has two hidden shafts, and an intriguing niche, with a short shaft leading off from it.

But the acolyte, in proceeding along inside this vast building, holding his torch of burning oil or pitch, upon reaching the end of the Ascending Passage, did not have to proceed on the level towards the Queen's Chamber. Instead, if he looked up overhead, he could discover a low wall giving access to the ascending walkway of the Grand Gallery. Then he or she would, after some arduous effort, clamber up onto it, and walk along this elevated walkway, past the three stone slabs which would later be used to plug the Ascending Passage.

Eventually at the end of the Grand Gallery, the acolyte would need to take one huge last step, then bend over to get into some small chambers, and negotiating through these, finally enter the remarkable King's Chamber. (Illustration 10) Waiting there was an empty ceremonial sarcophagus. As we shall see, the internal structure of the Great Pyramid is in fact an architectural metaphor, paralleling the spiritual journey of the acolyte up to higher realms.

The three-day spiritual sleep.
Now lets get a little more acquainted with the idea of the main ancient religious rite for the priests. We noted earlier how in ancient times in all cultures, there was an intense interest in attaining some form of interaction with higher realities and the gods, and the priesthoods used a variety of techniques to achieve this. Now we need to just remind ourselves that to the ancients, being asleep meant being out of the body, i.e., leaving the body. Thus the sleeper was, by default, in spirit realms. The ancient Greeks referred to sleep as the little brother of death, because in death one left the body in a permanent way, remaining in those spiritual realms, whereas in sleep one came back to the body each morning.

Now it is not only in this great sacred site that a mysterious sarcophagus is to be found; they are also found in old Celtic sites. In ancient times an acolyte would be placed in a stone sarcophagus as part of the initiation process. Then an artificially induced sleep condition would allow the soul to be set free from the body, and to journey into the spiritual realms.[39]

During this time, the acolyte would descend into the Underworld, which is the matrix of the human soul, and gain a clear, objective view of his or her own lower self. Hellenistic Greek documents indicate that there was also a process, called an anabasis, wherein the acolyte ascended up to the divine beings from whom the human spirit derives. To the ancient Egyptians it was the sun spirit or the sun god Ra, also known as Osiris. The soul of the deceased strove to find its way up to the realm of the sun god, Osiris. This was the great drama that unfolds in the elaborate and intriguing texts of the Egyptian Book of the Dead.

There is very little in the way of written explanation of the details of this process, because all aspects of the old spiritual process were traditionally kept confidential. But this process is referred to in veiled language in Biblical texts and in Celtic literature of the British Isles. The famous story of the Hebrew mystic Jonah, the prophet who was swallowed by a whale and then three-days later was spat out onto the seashore, may be seen as a disguised way of telling those in the know about just this very process.

The whale symbolizes the spirit world. This esoteric interpretation of the legend of Jonah is not baseless; there is solid evidence in the Biblical story itself. For in the words which Jonah speaks whilst in his experience, in his prayer to God for help, there are some strange references, carefully intermingled with more normal imagery. He says;

> ...From the depths of Sheol, I called for help, and you listened to my cry. You hurled me into the deep, into the

---

[39] The spiritual thinker, Rudolf Steiner, commented on this process in his many books.

very heart of the seas, and the currents swirled about me; all your waves and breakers swept over me…in the troughs of mountains I was sinking into a realm whose bars would hold me forever. But you brought my life up from the pit, O Lord my God. (Book of Jonah 2:2-6)

Firstly, Jonah identifies his location as the Underworld, the realm of the Dead, for the term Sheol is the Hebrew name for the realm of the Dead! It is not the term of the insides of a whale. This esoteric interpretation which sees it as a description of a spiritual process, is directly affirmed by a spiritual text from Celtic Britain. It is in a poem, apparently written by King Urien Rheged, ruler of Cumbria in the 6th Century AD. Rheged was a prominent person in the mystical traditions of his times.

This king was the patron of the initiate bard Taliesin, who was probably in residence at his court. In his poem he asks the question, " Who brought Jonah out of Kyd?"[40] The term Kyd is short for Kyridwen or Keridwen; this is the Celtic name for the realm of the dead and its spirits, and also for the goddess ruling this realm.

So, Urien Rheged has concluded that the story of Jonah is about the spiritual process that involves a descent into the Underworld, in a kind of soul journey. We noted earlier the secret underground chamber on the plateau where a sarcophagus was found in a chamber with water around it. It may well be that the feature of having water surrounding the sarcophagus here (coming in from the Nile River), was designed to symbolize the same situation that the symbolic story of Jonah presents. It is as if the acolyte deep down in the Osiris Chamber would arise out of a sea, out of the Underworld.

So, a sarcophagus in such a remarkable monument as the Great Pyramid may reasonably be considered to be part of an

[40] E. Davies, trans. & editor, The mythology and rites of the British Druids, J. Booth, London, 1809 p. 409.

initiatory process. It is then reasonable to conclude that to enter the Great Pyramid, and to make your way up into King's Chamber, is to be entering a very special place, reserved for those persons being initiated.

So bear in mind as you stand in the King's Chamber that here long ago, it is quite possible that acolytes were placed in the sarcophagus for three-days and nights (like Jonah in the whale). And they would then, after some undisclosed spiritual experience, be awakened to arise as an enlightened soul. There are other sites which also were designed to facilitate some form of spiritual awakening, or initiation, including the three-day sleep. But none of these other sites can claim such greatness in terms of engineering feats as the Great Pyramid.

We cannot know precisely what happened in the chamber, as these processes and rituals, which enabled a person to have such an experience, were kept strictly secret. But it seems from indications about the spiritual path in antiquity that only after arduous training could someone hope to enter the three-day sleep, such as was carried out in the so-called King's Chamber. Perhaps this room, with its five layers of granite ceilings above the sarcophagus, is much more accurately titled The Upper Initiation Chamber, see illustration 11. And something similar probably occurred at the underground Osiris Chamber.

From the scanty references to this in ancient literature, it can be concluded that the ancient Egyptians believed that the acolyte who underwent initiation in this chamber experienced the divine higher realms, and also sublime spiritual beings whom they perceived as guiding human destiny. This is the reason why the Great Pyramid was built with such unusual internal rooms and corridors, creating a metaphorical story in stone for the acolyte to read. Let's now consider some other main points which one needs to know to really appreciate the Great Pyramid.

8 The Descending Passage Going down 107 metres to the ground beneath the Great Pyramid, carved out with extreme precision

9 ARCHITECTURE AS STORYLINE:

Is this the spiritual message of the Great Pyramid? A depiction of both the after-life journey and also the related process of initiation.

1 The Parting of the Ways; down to darkness or up to light?

2 Down into dismal realms.

3 Realm of Seth, a metaphor for Hell, with false exits and dead-end pits.

4 The right path, towards the light.

5 Slipping backwards; a moral fall still possible.

6 The deceased finds a provisional home. First success for the acolyte;

7 The real ascent; difficult, but leads to realm of Osiris.

8 Nearly there; a final large step and 3 confined spaces as last barrier to the divine.

9 The good deceased soul enters Osiris' Kingdom. The acolyte enters the 3 day sleep'; air shafts permit breathing.

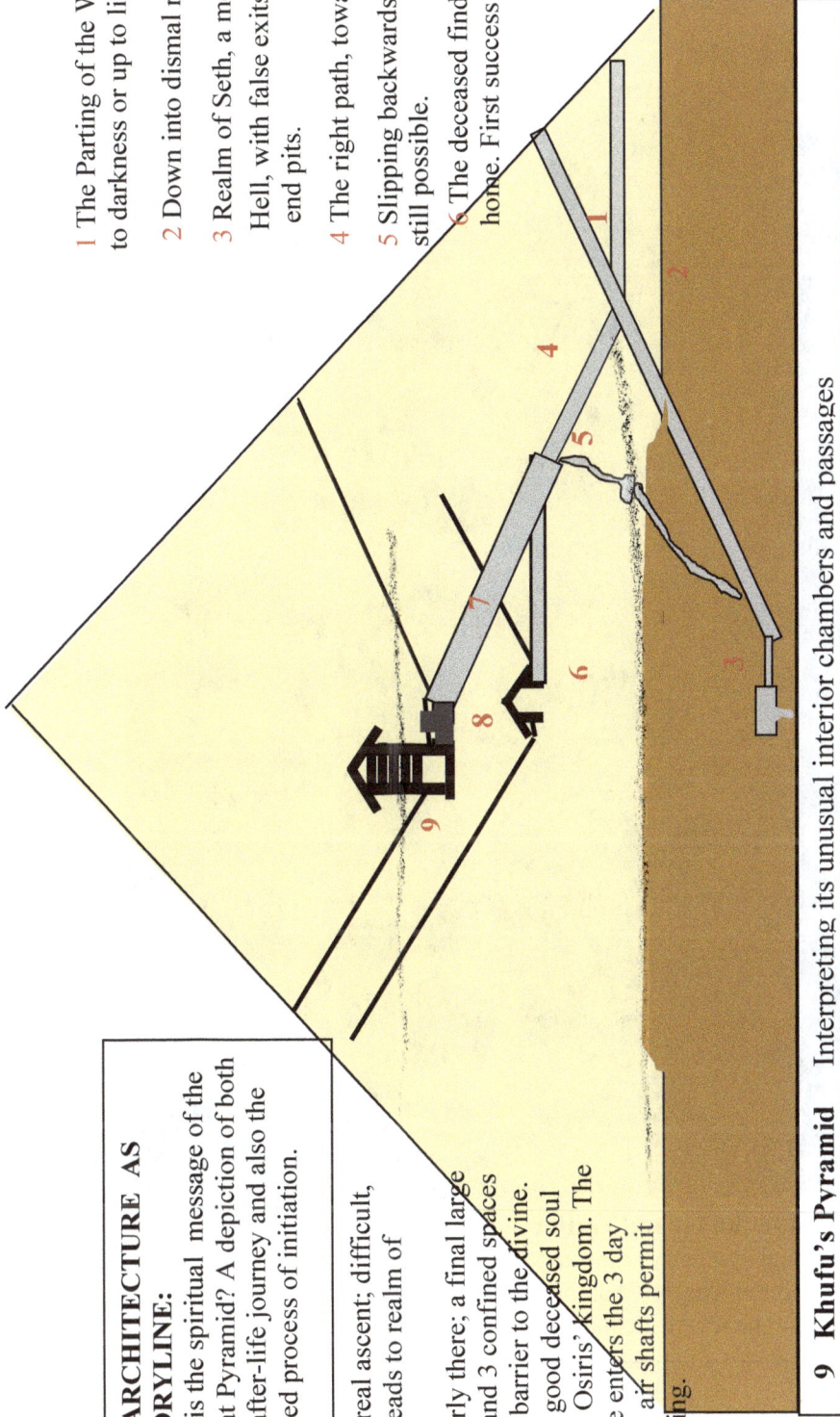

9 Khufu's Pyramid   Interpreting its unusual interior chambers and passages

10 Inside the Grand Gallery
The actual low entry point into the tiny ante-rooms which give access to the King's Chamber. The photo had to be over-exposed, to enable the lower section to be visible in our picture.

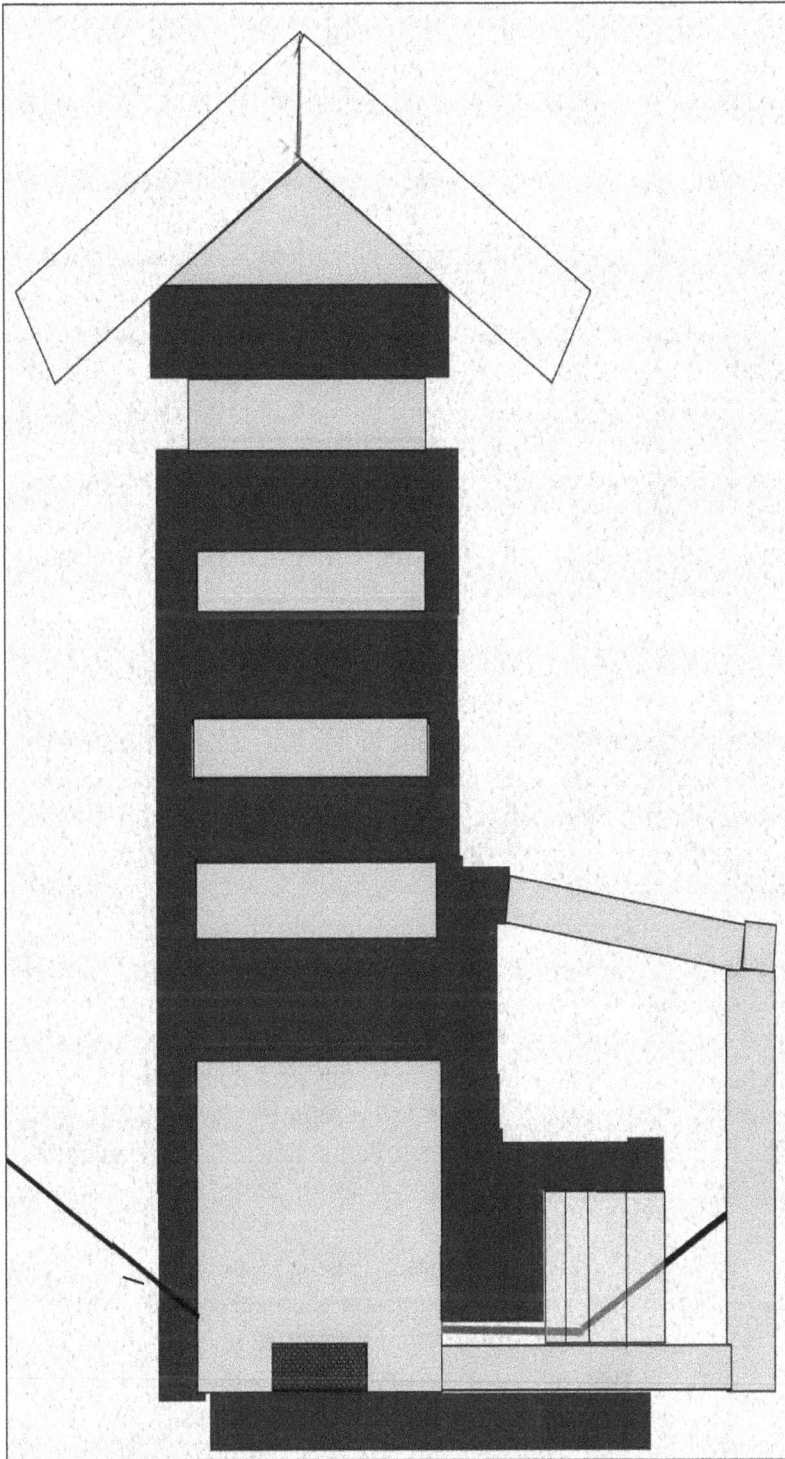

11 **The King's Chamber** Inside the limestone interior of the Great Pyramid, huge slabs of granite were used to create this special chamber with its 5 layered-ceiling, granite lidless sarcophagus, and 2 air shafts.

Chapter Seven Further secrets of the Great Pyramid

The cosmic correspondences: why is it shaped as a pyramid?

Now we need to consider the question, why is the pyramidal shape used in Egypt and elsewhere? It is important to note here that in fact, as regards Egyptian architecture, there is not one, but two, reasons for the pyramidal shape. Lets deal with the simpler reason first. A number of earlier Egyptian pyramids were not smooth but stepped, that is, they did not have smooth walls, but went up in stages, in seven stages. We noted earlier that a pyramidal tomb at Meidum which had been built as a seven-tiered monument, was later converted into a normal, smooth-walled pyramid.

The stepped, seven layers pyramid shape had its origin in the same attitude that created the Tibetan stupas, and the Babylonian ziggurats: namely that in the religions of these and many other lands, the spiritual realms are seven in number. By building such monuments, the populace would have their attention directed towards these seven realms of the after-life.

So, when people gazed at a sacred temple, from the vast flat plains of the Mesopotamian region, or from the flat flood plains of the Nile, they would see a tangible sign of the seven higher realms. The same method was adopted in Christian churches, where a cross, high on the top of a church spire as a symbol of Christ's sacrifice, could be seen by the populace for miles around. But why was the seven-stage ziggurat replaced by the pyramid shape with smooth sloping walls?

This is quite a difficult question, as no specific text has survived from the ancient Egyptians themselves, to explain this. So insight into the more extended, more holistic attitudes of antiquity is needed. In mainstream archaeology, there are various theories about this. For example, a pyramid text (no. 267), written on the walls of a 5th dynasty pyramid, is referred to. It says of the deceased Pharaoh lying inside, "A staircase to heaven is laid for him, so that he may mount up to heaven thereby." And an additional text referred to is an Egyptian magical spell, no. 508 in the pyramid texts, which states that Ra, in speaking to the pharaoh in his pyramidal tomb, "Ra says that Heaven has strengthened for you the rays of the sun, in order that you may lift yourself up towards the sun."

Based on such sparse words, the conclusion was reached by Egyptologists that the pyramid is an earthly manifestation of the sun, and its rays. So by being placed inside the pyramid, whose sides glow in a manner similar to the radiant sun, and at a similar angle to the slanting rays of the sun, the pharaoh in his pyramid was already in the sun, in the realm of Ra (or Osiris).

Although we feel that this conclusion has some basis to it, there is surely more to the use of the pyramid shape than this. At Heliopolis it was taught that the Earth at the beginning of time was pyramidal, and from this arose the tradition of making the ritual object known as a ben-ben stone or a pyramidion, and from this the pyramid as such was created.

So the Earth was created by, or with the help of, Ra the sun god, but it is still the Earth, it is not the realm of the sun god. Our view is that the above brief texts refer firstly to the general orientation of the pyramid, which surges upwards, heavenwards, similar to a ziggurat. So, "A staircase to heaven is laid for him, so that he may mount up to heaven thereby", means that the pyramid, despite being smooth, is still a kind of upwards-towering form, helping taking the soul up to the heavens. And in addition it means that the great power of the sun god, his influence within the realm of matter, has created the pyramidal shape.

So whilst it is an earthly dwelling, it is permeated by the creative power of the solar deity. For the pyramidal shape of the Earth was created by Ra. So from the viewpoint of the ancient Egyptian priests, the pyramid is a shape which results when the sun god asserts his divine power over the earth forces. From the effect of these two factors, the pyramid could be seen as a stairway to heaven, having its own inherent link to the sun god. But furthermore there is an inscription mentioned by Dr. Hawass, from the pyramidion of pharaoh Amenememhet III, which reads,

> "May the face of the king be opened, so that he may see the Lord of Heaven (i.e, Harakhte) when he crosses the sky; may he cause the king to chime* as a god, lord of eternity and indestructible" Harakhte replies that, 'He has given the beautiful portal to the king.'" [41]
> {*resonate is a better term here.}

This text affirms our interpretation of the use of a pyramid shape. It is more natural to view it as referring to the pharaoh gazing up beyond the pinnacle of this pyramid and beholding the sun disc overhead; rather than to seeing the sun god <u>inside</u> the pyramid. The pyramid is not the sun god, as such. It is unlikely that the pharaoh would see the perfection of the sun god by gazing around inside the pyramid. Nor is it likely that the text means that the pharaoh would see the bright walls of the pyramid as the sun god.

The pyramid shape was used because it was a symbol of an earthly home, but one which is permeated by the divine sun god, Ra. If you are inside a pyramid, then you are somehow near to the sun god; and that is exactly what the deceased yearns for. Just as the primordial pyramidal Earth came from the creative powers of the sun god in the Day of Creation. And furthermore, the pyramid also towers heavenwards as did the ziggurat. So the pyramid text is a plea that the pharaoh may gaze up from the top of the pyramid and see the sun disc high up in the sky, "May he resonate with the divine sun god." So in effect it is a prayer based on the idea that the pyramid-shaped tomb can naturally facilitate this experience.

---

[41] www.guardians.net/Hawass/mortuary1. Note: "the beautiful <u>portal</u> to the king" is my version, the original having "<u>horizon</u>" .

Now it is quite possible that the priests actually viewed the Earth itself as pyramidal, and this was another reason why the pharaohs created the pyramids. We have seen that it is very likely that people in earlier ages believed in, and even had a capacity to sense, subtle energies. If this is so, then it is very likely that in earlier ages the underlying geometric form of the Earth was considered to be a pyramid and not the obvious round global shape. For the huge segments or plates which make up Earth's crust do tend to have an underlying tetrahedral or pyramidal shape, a shape which has become rounded out by the activity of celestial forces operative from the solar system.

This fact has been noted by geologists, such Green, Moreux and Wegener, back in the 19th century, and by others in recent years. They noted that the large slabs of the Earth's surface (known as tectonic plates) that make up the crust of the Earth, may have first formed into a tetrahedron, a pyramid shape, as the planet was forming, before being rounded out, finally becoming a globe. Then the resulting planet would be a pear-shaped globe, the thinner top part being the after-effect of the pointed top of the pyramid, and the larger bottom area being the after-effect of the flat underside of the pyramidal form. And our planet is in fact a slightly pear-shaped globe.

Very recently this old view of the Earth's crust as being something which tends towards a pyramidal form, which becomes rounded out because of external forces acting upon it, was again put forward by modern scientists, by two geologists in Australia. (22) They point out that the structure of the tectonic plate of our planet is theoretically pyramidal. The possibility exists that somehow in past ages the priesthoods perceived this same situation. To them the Earth was in essence pyramidal shaped.

This is probably the reason why pyramids have been built all over the Earth, for pyramids are not only Egyptian. Archaeologists have uncovered many other pyramids, even if made only from shaped mounds of earth, in China, Greece, in

South America. And in New Age literature, reports exist of natural hills being shaped into pyramidal forms, in various countries around the world. Just as earlier peoples often shaped their dwellings or settlements to conform to features of their micro-ecology, so too, the priesthood of antiquity shaped their temples into a pyramid form, the core shape of the macro-ecology; namely the shape of the Earth's tectonic plates.

We can also note here that the crust of the Earth, from which the tectonic plates are formed is made up of 70% silica; and each silica crystal is a tiny tetrahedron or pyramid, in shape! The holistic sensing of the Earth by ancient peoples may have brought forth a feeling of a large pyramidal form, itself made up of a vast quantity of crystalline pyramidal forms. Now at this point you might think that we have covered most of the mysteries about the Great Pyramid, but not so, there is more to explore.

The purpose of the Pyramid's mysterious shafts
We noted earlier how the four walls of the Great Pyramid are divided subtly into two sides, making the pyramid reflect back the sunlight when the sun rises, as the equinoxes draw near. Quite a remarkable statement for a monument to make! But was there also a link between the Great Pyramid and the heavens for people who were **inside** the monument; in other words, did the shafts from the initiatory chambers make a connecting link somehow? This brings us to the fascinating theme of the shafts. There are four mysterious shafts incorporated into the interior of the building. Two of these proceed from the so-called Queen's Chamber and two from the King's Chamber.

As Rudolf Gantenbrink points out, the two shafts leading from the lower chamber (Queen's Chamber) do not now, and never did, meet the open air; that is, they do not proceed all the way through the pyramid to the outside. And the two shafts leading out of the King's Chamber, while they do proceed through to the outside, were probably closed-over most of the time. (23)

His site is very informative, (www.cheops.org). Sophisticated 3D drawings (CAD format) allow you to see the chambers and passages of the pyramid, extremely well.

The shafts manoeuvre their way around obstacles, such as the ceiling of the Grand Gallery. This is very important! No starlight could ever penetrate either chamber along these bent shafts, even if they were ever open to the outside. But the two shafts from the upper chamber do reach to the outside, and thus could be designed to symbolically provide a pathway for the soul to find its way up to the cosmos. But if they were left uncovered permanently, then vermin and dust etc, would have entered, despoiling the special chamber.

A very pragmatic purpose of the shafts in the upper chamber was revealed when they were cleaned out in the 19th century, after millennia of disuse, and a draught of cold air entered into the chamber, resulting in a pleasant air temperature being constantly maintained in the chamber. So, their pragmatic purpose was that of providing air. But we note here that fresh air is only provided for living people, **not a mummy**! The air-flow enabled anyone who was in there, for example, for spiritual purposes, to breathe.

However, the two shafts in the lower chamber are most intriguing; they are blocked, that is, they do not go all the way to the outside. But in addition, each of these shafts, which are only 8 inches wide (20 cms), actually come to an end, high up inside the pyramid in a tiny hinged slab (not really a door) made of polished limestone; and behind this is another such slab! Further investigation has revealed that behind the second slab with its copper handles, is an empty space blocked by a piece of limestone, somewhat cracked. Although there was much hype in the world's press about a possible secret room, this is most unlikely.

It is very unlikely indeed that a secret room is hidden up there, as we are now near to the outside of the pyramid, and with an entrance only wide enough for a cat. For a really detailed examination of the shafts, see the very clear presentation by the website of Zahi Hawass. (24) This site has a link to the site of Rudolf Ganzenbrink.

Now these two shafts in the lower chamber are simply astonishing. For they never let anything in, neither air nor starlight. Because they stop before the outer layer of the pyramid, they do not go to the outside. But also they only commence from some 5 inches (8 cm) **inside the stone walls of the Queens' Chamber**! So they don't start from the interior of the chamber at all, they start **from inside** the stone wall. In fact no one in that chamber would know that they were even there, as they were hidden, and were only discovered by accident. We shall look again at these two lower shafts, later.

Now, it is also the case that to build up a huge pyramid in horizontal levels of stone slabs, and then to run four diagonal shafts through these levels, is to impose an enormous technical problem on the builders. These narrow shafts, if they had not been very painstakingly integrated into the many courses of limestone blocks, would have caused the internal structure of the chambers below to collapse. So they are obviously important, but their purpose is still unclear. Mainstream scholars conclude that they are to do with the after-death beliefs of the ancient Egyptians, namely to allow the soul of the deceased Pharaoh to ascend up to certain stars, as referred to in the funeral texts. And in so far as the pyramid is also probably the tomb of Khufu, this would be one of two functions of these shafts.

Very occasionally a mainstream researcher, such as an astronomer, may suggest that a way to date the monument is by considering these shafts, and whether they are aligned to any prominent star in some previous century. We have noted how this was done in regard to the alignment of the Descending Passage. Some mainstream researchers offer the date of 2,170 BCE as the date of the pyramid's construction, because of an alignment with a star and this passage then; but this is far too recent a date for the building of the Great

Pyramid. So, generally, the mainstream approach is not to emphasise this star alignment as of pivotal value in dating the monument. So why were these shafts built?

There is no alignment of the shafts to a group of stars
Both mainstream and alternative writers who know that the shafts don't lead to the outside, and hence have no alignment with stars, view them as purely a theoretical feature, designed to highlight the cosmic perspective on life embedded in ancient Egyptian religions. To these scholars, the alignment has been arranged in order to meet the needs of the pharaoh Khufu after death, and hence possibly could be a way to date the pyramid. This brings us to the ideas about the shafts, especially the two upper ones, from New Age researchers. Their arguments centre on the alignment of the shafts to certain stars in earlier ages.

To these New Age writers, there is an alignment and it is there to ensure that the new building really manifests the cosmic link between the deceased, the gods and the stars, i.e., for people living at the time of its construction. And therefore this definitely does allow one to date the pyramid. So with these writers, the alignment is not due to the need of the deceased Pharaoh Khufu, as he journeys up into the heavens. The alignment is there, they say, because the new pyramid had to be involved with the stars and their role in the after-life in general. But it soon becomes apparent that this theory has no basis to it.

Was there an intention to coincide the construction of the Great Pyramid to some star alignments? Can one date the Great Pyramid by finding star alignments, and why would such alignments be so pivotal? Firstly, as we noted earlier, the shafts in the lower chamber are totally enclosed, so there can be no question of any physical sighting of a star. And the shafts in the upper chamber were often closed, but perhaps opened for special occurrences. New Age authors make detailed projections onto star maps of the angle of the shafts, dated to earlier millennia, to show that these shafts were aligned to stars in the constellations of Orion and Draco and the Little Bear.

Their focus is on the constellation of Orion in particular, because the three pyramids at Giza roughly form a reflection of the three central stars in the constellation of Orion. The theory is that at certain times in the ancient past, especially at ca. 9,000 BC, there were alignments of specific important stars to these shafts. At this time, it is claimed, in the lower chamber the northern shaft was aligned with a star in the constellation of Little Bear (Beta Ursa Minor), and the southern shaft was aligned with the great star Sirius. (Even though these shafts are totally blind, do not go through to the sky.) Whereas in the upper chamber, it is claimed, the southern shaft was aligned to a star in Orion (Zeta Orionis), and the northern shaft with a star in Draco (Alpha Draconis), which was at that time the Pole star.

However, we note here that since the shafts are bent, there could be no sighting or alignment with a star, at any time. Once you know this, then what appears at first to be a reasonable idea, is no longer viable at all. Furthermore, Frank Dörnenburg has shown that this entire "discovery" is without any foundation. The angles of these shafts were measured in a scientific research project, by the engineer Gantenbrink, and one has to use the correct scientific data which resulted from his work, when trying to see if any alignment occurred with a star. But as Dörnenburg shows, by using the correct calculations, the date of about 9,200 BC is without any basis. These shafts would be in alignment with only one of the stars mentioned, for a few decades, but they could only become aligned to another of these stars some 250 years later!

The entire argument is baseless. To get all four stars into alignment with their shaft, one would have to sit there, waiting over a period of some 300 years, as one by one they came into, and went out of alignment; a meaningless situation. So, the Great Pyramid shafts were not in alignment with these four stars. They were never in alignment with these four stars at the same time.

What about Orion? Are the three pyramids, in their position on the sandy plateau, in alignment with the three central stars of Orion? Dörnenburg shows clearly that, scientifically speaking, they are not a true reflection of the three stars, in terms of their precisely calculated respective brightness and positions. Also they are not a mirror image of the three stars, i.e., they are not an accurate carbon copy of the pattern that these three stars make in the sky. Certainly, if the three pyramids are to truly represent the three stars, then they should be a carbon copy, that is, a reversed mirror image of them, not a simple direct copy. That is, as Dornenburg argues, for the pyramids to accurately reflect the stars of Orion, they have be **a reversal** of how the stars appear in the sky, because they are being projected onto the ground, thus automatically becoming a mirror image.

This statement from Dornenburg that the three pyramids are not designed to be a reflection of the central stars of Orion, because they do not appear as a true reversal or carbon copy of the stars, is scientifically accurate. But it is probably incorrectly applied here. We need to see that his line of reasoning is very much derived from our modern attitudes. It is in fact reasonable to conclude that the three pyramids could have been designed so as to appear as a rough replica of the three stars in Orion's belt – but in a simple and direct way, leaving out the need to change them into a mirror image.

This sort of simplified arrangement would have been right to undertake for people of nearly 5000 years ago, when the mindset was less scientifically oriented than it is today. The way the world was seen long ago was not so aligned to the physical perspective and spatial proportions as it is today. A study of art history reveals just how little the people of that era were focussed on, or even aware of, correct perspective (i.e., on the precise way in which surfaces and proportions actually are seen by the eye, over distances).

In this sense, the three pyramids are indeed similar to the three stars of Orion; to a simple way of thinking, which ignores the technical need for a mirror image. Of course, there would have to be a reason for doing this in the first place, but such a reason could be found, in a general sense, in the focus on the cosmos by people of the Mesopotamian-Egyptian age. This point that in ancient times an approximation was appropriate for the general populace, is quite relevant. However, this entire point actually means that this idea of building three pyramids so as to reflect the bright stars in the belt of Orion, was undertaken by Khufu and was then deliberately and faithfully carried out over the next two generations, by his son and grandson.

It is one thing for three pyramids to be built to a special pattern within the one construction project. But since it is now clearly established that they were built by three generations of Egyptians in the Old Kingdom, this idea would mean that the grand scheme was carried out specifically by the descendants of Khufu. This is unusual, but not impossible. And there is in fact some evidence that these three generations did agree to complete this grand scheme. When Menkaure built his pyramid, he placed the causeway, leading down towards the Nile, and also the valley temple, in such a way as to <u>block access onto the Giza plateau for any later large-scale building project</u>.

Another example of how the Great Pyramid could have been designed to be a kind of reflection in miniature of the cosmos, applies to another claim about special cosmic dimensions of the Great Pyramid, namely, that the height of the pyramid when multiplied by one thousand million, gives the distance of the Sun to the Earth. Now, scientifically it is known that due to the Earth having an elliptical path around the sun, not a round orbit, the distance of the Earth to the sun varies by some 3 million miles.

So naturally, the mainstream attitude here is that the above idea is just another false claim. And this is an understandable attitude for another reason, when you consider that modern science only determined the distance between the sun and the Earth in the 18th century (1761), using trigonometry and scientific astronomical research. And any suggestion that knowledge of this was possible about 5,000 years earlier would not be regarded as sensible. And furthermore, since the top of the pyramid is missing, its original precise height is impossible to prove.

However, despite all this, the claim that the Great Pyramid's dimensions are a reflection of the distance between the Earth and sun is a reasonable one. If this feature was designed as a basic statement about the over-all relationship of the sun to the Earth, ignoring this relatively small variation. And this is very likely, because a close approximation would be sufficient for people then, and such an approximation would have been effective for purely religious-symbolic purposes. But once again, we encounter a striking feature of research into ancient sites. If such claims are to be considered at all, then we have to accept that ancient priesthoods possessed a form of psychic ability for carrying out spiritual research, which gave them remarkable knowledge, which would not otherwise be accessible by scientific instruments for millennia to come.

CHAPTER Eight Giza and Khufu and initiation

Did Khufu build the Great Pyramid?

It is now time for us to look at the question of when was the Great Pyramid built, i.e., was it built under the authority of Pharaoh Khufu, about 2,800-2,600 BC? As we noted earlier, the accessible chambers of the Great Pyramid, like those of many other pyramids, are generally devoid of inscriptions or artworks which could allow one to positively identify the Pharaoh responsible for its construction. However, in 1837 a British military man, Howard Vyse, undertook explorations in the pyramid. He announced the crucial discovery of hieroglyphs in the sealed spaces within the five-fold ceiling compartments above the King's Chamber. Two of these included the name of Pharaoh Khufu! This discovery was a major breakthrough which allowed Egyptologists to conclude that it was built under Khufu's authority.

In the 1980's however, a New Age journalist, driven by ideas that UFO intelligences had been responsible for the Earth's cultural developments, began to spread the rumour that this discovery by Colonel Vyse was a fraud, and that the Great Pyramid was many millennia older. And the idea that these Giza monuments may derive from a now forgotten civilisation, in particular, from Atlantis, has also been a core idea amongst various mystical societies in the west. This theory has been put forward since the 19th century by various writers, on the basis of mystical convictions, such as H. P. Blavatsky, co-founder of the Theosophical Society, and the American trance medium Edgar Cayce.

These writers put forward the idea of Atlantis as a historical reality, an idea that is not invalid in itself, although much more evidence is needed for this to be acceptable to the mainstream academic world. But such writers, in pushing back the age of the Great Pyramid into the grey mists of so-called Atlantean pre-history, offer no solid basis for doing so. This idea was well received by a variety of mystical groups, and provided a basis for such writings. It is a romantic idea that has exerted a lot of influence on the popular imagination.[42] However, despite Cayce having made many accurate and very helpful medical diagnoses, not all of his statements (produced in a sleep state or trance state) were accurate. For example, his prophecy that the sunken island-continent of Atlantis would arise again out of the waters of the Atlantic Ocean, before the 1970's, failed to come true.

Those who want to persuade people that the monuments here are pre-diluvial, claim that Vyse had committed fraud. They claim that Vyse himself painted the hieroglyphs in the small spaces, to grab some glory and the consequent social and financial benefits. In particular it is argued that the hieroglyph for Khufu, as painted on the stone by Vyse (via an assistant) is both recently done, and also is incorrect; for it reads, not Khu-fu, but Ra-fu; which is a non-existent and absurd word. It is also claimed that an expert in Egyptology from the British Museum, a certain Samuel Birch, noticed serious inconsistencies in Vyse's report and his drawings of the discovered writings.

This expert, so it is said, reported that the hieroglyphs are actually so peculiar as to be impossible, coming from different times in Egyptian history, some deriving from a period hundreds of years after Khufu, etc. Naturally, this has added fuel to the fire for those who are seeking to find an Atlantean or at least pre-diluvial origin of the Great Pyramid.

So, do these hieroglyphs inside the Great Pyramid really have the name of Khufu on them, and are they ancient? The false nature of the claims has now been revealed. Careful research by Frank Dörnenburg and others, has now established that these critical statements, allegedly made by the expert Birch, in his assessment of the drawings submitted by Vyse, are in fact, totally non-existent. They are not in the Birch report! In Birch's report, one finds no reasons whatsoever to doubt the

---

[42] A rare voice in western mystical circles who taught that the Sphinx and Great Pyramid were constructed in old Egypt, is the Austrian spiritual writer Rudolf Steiner, who broke away from the Theosophists in 1912.

validity of the hieroglyphs discovered by Vyse. Finally, the claim that Vyse had committed fraud and had been consequently exposed by Mr. Birch, is quite wrong, as Dörnenburg points out. The actual fact is, that the assessment written up by Samuel Birch of the drawings, made by Vyse, is published in a book about the great discovery, **written by Vyse himself**, some years later! You can be assured that this assessment does not make a fool or a knave out of Vyse. It confirms the accuracy of the discovery; it does not discredit him. Dornenburg's website is really worthwhile visiting, (http://doernenburg.alien.de/RDV).

It is an undeniable fact that the royal cartouche of Pharaoh Khufu, and other old Egyptian words have been written on a stone block up in the inaccessible area above the multi-layered ceiling of the King's Chamber. Words have been written in Egyptian hieroglyphs on these stone slabs, following the Egyptian custom of marking various stone slabs to indicate the work-gang whose responsibility they were, or for which site they were intended, etc.

The cartouche of Khufu is not a modern fake, it was written when the pyramid was being built, nearly 5,000 years ago, as the red ochre has become covered in minute crystals, which condensed over the ochre in the course of millennia. And indeed part of the perimeter of one of these cartouches of pharaoh Khufu actually extends around on to the end of a slab, and has become blocked from sight, by the next stone placed tightly against it.

So the cartouche of Khufu is real, and yes, it does date from the time the Great Pyramid was constructed, see illustration 12. Further evidence that Khufu built the Great Pyramid is also available. Cartouches of his name are being found in other sites, on rocks which have been taken to be re-used for the building of another pyramid or tomb, such as the pyramid of Amenemhat I at Lisht, some 50kms away from Giza. Furthermore, cartouches of Khufu have been found in artwork from much later dynasties, for example, the lovely golden

"Ring of Cheops", from the 25th dynasty, and many scarabs inscribed with his cartouche from the 26th dynasty, show that this pharaoh was held in very high esteem, and was deified in later millennia. The presence of the cartouche of pharaoh Khufu, found high up, in a cavity in the pyramid, is real proof that Pharaoh Khufu had the Great Pyramid built. But people still ask, is it?

The idea that the Great Pyramid is very ancient, originating in a pre-Flood epoch, is still believed by many people. So, to these people the Khufu cartouche, found in the upper area of the pyramid is just not acceptable. Does the fact that the Khufu cartouche actually exists in the Great Pyramid mean anything at all?

The truth of this inscription has a crucial significance. Could this also be just another red herring, as some people argue? There are people who wish to argue away the discovery of the name of the pharaoh Khufu in the Great Pyramid. A good example of just how ingrained is the idea that the Great Pyramid must be Atlantean or at least extremely old, and therefore the cartouche must be rejected, is found in the reaction of Schoch, the geologist who claims that the sphinx dates back many millennia before Khufu.

He was so determined to expose the cartouche as nonsense that he gained permission to physically inspect the hieroglyphs in the cramped spaces above the King's Chamber. He wrote that in fact, there are small crystal deposits which have formed over the ochre writing, and this proves them to be authentic, to be very old indeed. So he had to admit that they are not forgeries.

But then, amazingly, he mentions that in a lower space there is another hieroglyph which spells out Khnum-Khufu, implying he says, "that the other term, Khnum-Khufu, is perhaps the name of a god". Thereby putting into doubt that these two names refer to the historical pharaoh, Khufu. So, the question arises here, could the cartouche of Khufu be a red herring?

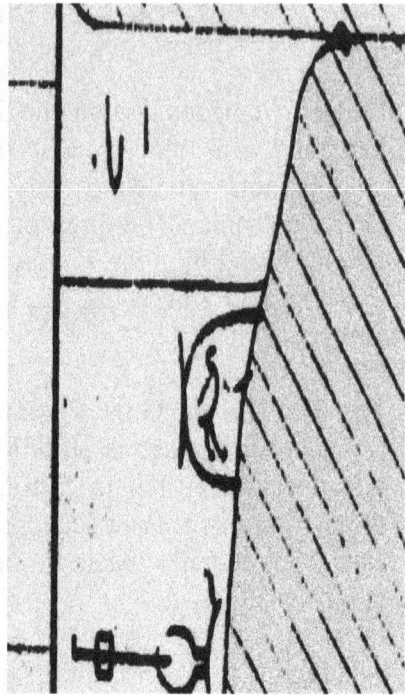

12 The Cartouche of Khufu in the narrow   spaces above the King's Chamber

Left: A photo of an authentic cartouche of Khufu inside the great pyramid, from the time it was built. Above: Another cartouche of Khufu which extends behind a second large rock slab which was placed by the pyramid builders at the time the pyramid was built, thus partly obscuring the other cartouche.

These hieroglyphs spell out the cartouche of Pharaoh Khufu, they are not fakes.

(F r o m F. Doernenburg, colorized for clarity)

Was it put there by pre-diluvial people and does not refer to the Old Kingdom pharaoh Khufu at all? Now the situation is that Khnum is indeed the name of a god, but Khnum-Khufu is the name of the pharaoh Khufu. It is one of five titles or names which pharaohs were given, and means "the god Khnum protects me". Inscriptions exist elsewhere, from military campaigns undertaken by Khufu, where he is also addressed as Khnum-Khufu. What is so important is that this name inside the Great Pyramid is written as a cartouche, that is, it designates a pharaoh; so it simply cannot be referring to a god. It has to refer to a pharaoh.

Careful research has shown that it cannot be dismissed; it is not a modern forgery. And as Dr. Hawass points out, part of the cartouche goes around the side of a stone slab, and is hidden by the adjoining slab. So the cartouche was written on the stone before the pyramid was built. Hence Schoch's hinting remark is quite irrelevant and disappointing; it shows that the yearning for an Atlantean origin is irresistible.

Another way in which the discovery of the name of the pharaoh Khufu in the Great Pyramid is argued away, is by saying that the pyramid itself was called Khnum-Khufu, and that the Pharaoh was named after the pyramid. This is obviously false, since the pyramid is known in Egyptian texts as the Horizon of Khufu, and never associated with Khnum. Khufu also has four other specific titles, in accordance with Egyptian tradition, and one of them is Khnum-Khufu.

The inconsistencies of a pre-diluvial Great Pyramid
Finally, we have to consider once more whether, despite all of the above facts this cartouche is pre-Egyptian, and derives from some pre-diluvial civilisation, such as the fabled Atlantean people. The idea of Atlantis or another pre-diluvial civilization as such, is not inherently false nor unscientific. But to believe that the hieroglyphics above the King's Chamber are Atlantean is absurd. This means that one believes that an advanced, pre-diluvial civilisation **wrote in Egyptian**

hieroglyphics about 10,000 BC, or 60,000 BC if one believes Blavatsky. But this also means that these Atlantean people, or some other very ancient civilisation, **only wrote in Egyptian hieroglyphics when they colonized Egypt** (and built monuments on the Giza plateau). Elsewhere, in their other colonies in other parts of the world, the Atlanteans used a different language. (!) For enigmatic pre-diluvial artefacts have been found in various countries around the world, but none of these have Egyptian hieroglyphics on them.

So this belief that the hieroglyphs inside the Great Pyramid are not from ancient Egypt, would mean that a pre-diluvial civilisation wrote in Egyptian hieroglyphics, but only in Egypt, and not in their other colonies. And also, that they had the very same cartouches as the pharaohs of the Old Kingdom. Or perhaps one believes that the pharaoh adopted a pre-flood term for his name, without ever indicating that it was such a special ancient term. These are all most unlikely conclusions. It also means that a very old, pre-flood Egyptian civilisation which already had hieroglyphs, left no other writings in all of Egypt, other than a few inscriptions, made by work-gangs inside the Great Pyramid.

Furthermore, the style of hieroglyphs inside the Great Pyramid is hieratic, an advanced form of writing, first developed in the Old Kingdom of Egypt. It is simpler and clearer than the type of hieroglyphs used some centuries earlier. Yet, these theoretical pre-diluvial people must have used this form of writing, which wasn't developed until about 8,000 years later. It is obvious that these beliefs fly in the face of rational thought. Archaeological and linguistic research is supportive of the view that the hieroglyphs were created in Egypt, some centuries before the time of Khufu.

The Great Pyramid was built by pharaoh Khufu in Egypt's Old Kingdom. And the great Sphinx and the pyramid of Khafre, which imitates the design of the Great Pyramid, were built in the Old Kingdom, and probably by Khafre. These monuments were all obviously constructed in the same general timeframe.

So, why are the pyramids so anonymous?
Since Khufu is the builder of the Great Pyramid, why is Khufu's name not prominently displayed in the Great Pyramid? You may be thinking that the evidence is actually very small, and that to establish who built the Great Pyramid has required some rather complex logic, and that is quite right. But strangely, most of the early pyramids are just as anonymous! For example, the famous Bent Pyramid of Meidum has no internal artwork to tell us who ordered its construction, and likewise with the other two large pyramids on Giza. The Bent Pyramid is ascribed to pharaoh Seneferu (Snofru) on the basis of a cartouche with his name found on a construction block, and a small amount of reliable evidence from later Egyptian texts.

Why the anonymity? Because the Great Pyramid was an embodiment of, or representation of, the primordial Day of Creation. Any plastering of a person's name over this monument would have been most inappropriate. As a monument designed to be used in spiritual processes this would also have been not correct protocol. Now compare these remarkably bare pyramids to actual burial chambers of the same epoch, with all their rich artwork. For example, the tomb of Khufu's mother, Hetep-heres I, or the tomb of Khufu's grand-daughter, Meresankh III, who was married to pharaoh Menkaure (Mycerinos), who built the smallest of the three Giza pyramids. In these burial sites, and many similar, the life and after-life of the deceased is depicted, usually with resplendent artwork.

Firstly, let's note here that the interior of all early Egyptian burial chambers were left bare, they were never decorated until the end of the 5th dynasty, ca. 2,300 BC. One factor here is that in antiquity the personality or the individual person, carrying out a task on behalf of the gods, was viewed as merely an agent of spiritual powers. This personality was not emphasized. For example, in this epoch (the Mesopotamian-Egyptian era) no artist ever signed his work of art, no matter how great it was. In the face of the sacred task being undertaken for the deified pharaoh and the gods, their personality was not significant. It would have been quite unthinkable for them to sign the work. It was not until the late Classical period of Greece that artists first began to sign their works.

This principle of not asserting one's own personal self was central to the attitudes of life in the Old Kingdom of Egypt, and no doubt all other ancient peoples. And when it came to the construction of an important monument, a monument intended to serve special spiritual-esoteric purposes, such as the Great Pyramid, this principle would be extended even further. Even the Pharaoh himself would not want his name emblazoned on such a building. But it is possible that such a place may then have been utilized as a tomb at some later era (we encounter this process with the fascinating Megalithic Newgrange Chamber in Ireland).

If a pyramid were designed to be much more than a burial site, in fact, designed to be used for initiation into the secrets of the sacred spiritual realities, then it would be the firm protocol that even the pharaoh did not seek to claim the credit for this monument. So the anonymous, bare interior of the Great Pyramid is not an enigma to those who understand ancient Egyptian cultural principles.

The connection of Khufu to the Great Pyramid, showing that he is its builder, is to be found in various old Egyptian texts. Ancient Egyptian texts refer to the pyramid as belonging to Khufu, (it is called the Realm of Khufu). Also a priest working in the associated mortuary temple was referred to as high priest of the realm of Khufu, and a senior building official is described as Supervisor of the realm of Khufu. But an even more significant text which links Khufu to the Great Pyramid, as a place with a secret spiritual purpose, is the very interesting "Westcar Papyrus". This ancient papyrus document speaks of a hidden esoteric wisdom that Khufu is seeking, in order to incorporate this hidden knowledge inside it. This affirms our conclusion that the principle of spiritual modesty, of not claiming credit, would be even stronger with the Great Pyramid than any other pyramid.

Khufu's pyramid and the Book of the sage Thoth (Hermes)
The Westcar Papyrus was found by a British collector (Westcar) in the 1830's and dates from about 1,600 BC. It is really very interesting because it directly states that the Pharaoh Khufu himself was searching for a secret known only to initiates of the Egyptian Mysteries, **so that he could construct the Great Pyramid according to spiritual wisdom**. Now of course, one can view this text as fictional narrative, but it is most unlikely that a fictional story from the Old Kingdom would take as its theme the Great Pyramid and the role of initiatory knowledge in its design. So it is very likely that a significant truth lies at the bottom of this account.

This ancient story tells of how Khufu was searching for secret documents (called Ipwt in hieroglyphics) of Hermes-Thoth, the founder of Egyptian spiritual wisdom, in order to design the interior chambers of the pyramid. The story was not seen in its deep spiritual implications by the Egyptologists at first, partly because a key hieroglyph for secret documents/designs presented linguistic problems, and another phrase about the chambers of Thoth, was not recognized in its full meaning for some decades. So, it was published in the 19th century as simply another entertaining folk-tale of the ancient Egyptians. (26)

Jenny Berggren's Master's Thesis, "The Ipwt in the Papyrus Westcar" provides an excellent analysis, and various translations of this text; she includes that of F.W. Green;

> 7,5-8 ...pharaoh also knows the number of the pDwt (the secret documents) of the chamber of Thoth. Now his majesty Khufu had been engaged for some time seeking for the ipwt nt wnt nt Dhwty (the secret documents of the god

Thoth) that he might make a copy thereof for his own tomb.[43]

Thoth is the supreme source of initiation wisdom in Egypt; a god who brought all the wisdom that enabled Egypt to arise to the great heights in the Old Kingdom. Thoth was not remote from the ancient priests; he could directly inspire them with this wisdom. One gains the impression from the Greek way of understanding Thoth that he spoke through a specific person, who was his mouthpiece, and who had written down this wisdom. Khufu is told of a mysterious sage called Ddy who knows the secret of these documents; and so he orders that the sage be brought to his court,

> … Khufu then says, "How about the report that you know the number of the secret documents of the chamber of Thoth?" Then Ddy said, "I know not the number thereof, O King, but I know the place they are in." Then his majesty said, "Where then?" Then Ddy said, "There is a flint box in the temple chamber called sipty in Heliopolis, it (or they) are in the box." 9;1-5.

Just what the ancient word, sipty means is unknown, but it is significant that this reference to secret wisdom obtained from Thoth, and being kept in a stone chest, also occurs in another ancient magical text from Egypt. As Berggren comments, although the last part of the Westcar papyrus is missing, it is very likely that Khufu eventually obtained the measurements, and that the internal plan of the Great Pyramid is an imitation of Thoth's secret chambers.

Now this is very valuable, as it gives an indication of the belief in ancient Egypt that the Great Pyramid does have an esoteric basis to its internal structure, deriving from the secret spiritual wisdom of Hermes.

---

[43] Jenny Berggren, The Ipwt Papyrus Westcar, Uppsala University Department of Archaeology and Ancient History & Egyptology: http://www.arkeologi.uu.se/egy/education/uppsatser/Berggren-Ipwt.pdf

The King's Chamber: key to a major purpose of the Great Pyramid

The reason, or rather the main reason among several reasons, for constructing the Great Pyramid, depends largely upon the purpose of the King's Chamber. We have already seen that there are great monuments on the Giza plateau which are not designed for the cult of the dead, but which have other spiritual-religious functions. We need to be open to the theoretical possibility of the Great Pyramid, and also Khafre's pyramid, having a primary function quite separate from a tomb.

It is important to note here, as we noted earlier, that there is a natural link between monuments designed as tombs, and temples designed to serve the spiritual quest of the priesthoods, for both the soul of the deceased and the mystic journey through the same spirit realms. Now we considered various features of the Great Pyramid which indicate that it was not designed for use as a tomb, and yet, like many tombs it is a pyramid.

It's really very important to remember at this point what we discovered about the reason for the pyramid shape being used in tombs, namely because it is a shape which **symbolises the powers of the sun god, active in matter.** We said then, "So this pyramid text is a plea that the pharaoh may gaze up from the top of the pyramid and see the sun disc high up in the sky, "May he resonate with the divine sun god." So in effect it is a prayer based on the idea **that the pyramid shaped tomb can naturally facilitate this ability to commune with the sun god.**"

And this is exactly the same goal for the acolyte during the three day religious rites, inside the Great Pyramid, where he is lying quietly in the sarcophagus, just as a deceased pharaoh's mummy lies quietly in his. He knew that he was inside a vast pyramidal shaped spiritual monument, so the spiritual energies of the sun god were surely being invoked, and supported him.

Above the ceiling of the King's Chamber there is a remarkable five-tiered ceiling. See illustration 11 for a clear diagram of the ceiling. This is normally described by Egyptologists as being designed to protect the chamber from the weight of the rest of the pyramid above it. But in the opinion of many people, this strange and obviously very important feature, is in fact putting huge weight upon the chamber. The weight factor of this five-tiered ceiling has been carefully examined, and some engineers have concluded that this multi-layered ceiling has caused some of the softer limestone slabs above the chamber to crack, and resulted in some of these slabs moving about 15cms under the weight.

Instead of relieving the weight, it is quite possible that this extraordinary multi-layered ceiling in fact is constantly applying weight to the roof of the King's Chamber. Engineers such as Gantenbrink have suggested that the strangely layered ceiling has nothing to do with taking the weight off the ceiling, but was necessary to prevent too much weight being placed on the southern end of the Grand Gallery. And yet its unusual multi-tiered design seems to point to something else as well, because relieving the weight on the structure below could have been achieved by a simple single-roofed chamber, as used in other Egyptian monuments. Five massive roofs or tiers were not needed for this.

The key to why the ceiling has these five layers is perhaps this: as we noted earlier in ancient times, the Earth was regarded in terms of the underlying geometry of its crust, to be a pyramid or tetrahedron (ignoring the later rounding-out). So, an acolyte undergoing some initiatory process deep in the Great Pyramid, was actually inside a scale model of the Earth itself.

The Egyptian priests may have concluded that this shape stimulated some subtle energy fields natural to the planet. They may have thought that placing a fivefold layering of granite above the sarcophagus would strengthen certain subtle earth energies to which the acolyte would be exposed. This unusual idea is given some credence by the fact that granite is used for these layers in the ceiling, not the usual limestone blocks from which the rest of the pyramid is built. Granite is also elsewhere used all around this special room.

As illustration 11 shows, the chamber walls are composed of huge slabs of granite, and so is the sarcophagus, and parts of the ante-chamber. Granite is a crystalline rock; it is known scientifically that granite, like any crystalline rock, has a natural capacity to respond to subtle energies. By which mainstream science means electro-magnetic rays of various kinds; but other energies not yet known to us today, are not excluded.

It is well established, though not fully accepted in mainstream circles, that other forms of energies also naturally exist in the world. These are referred to in various cultures as Ch'i or prana or in western terms, etheric energy. Was this five-layered ceiling in fact an architectural device designed to alter the naturally occurring earth-energies in such a way as to assist the person below, during an initiation process? We believe this may well have been part of the belief system of the ancient priesthood.

This view has some backing from scientific research. Tompkins mentions the fascinating news items that appeared in 1968, about attempts to take images of cosmic radiation from outer space, as it passed through the pyramid of Khafre. A large scientific team from the USA and the UAR, which involved the U.S. Atomic Energy Commission, set out to take images of the radiation. A leading scientist for the project, Dr. Amr Goneid of the Ein Shams University at Cairo, stated that the results obtained "defied all known laws of physics". A scientifically impossible maze of data had resulted which could not be explained.[44]

---

[44] P. Tompkins, Secrets of the Great Pyramid, Harper & Row, London, 1971, p.275

It is also the case that in the 1960's and 70's, Eastern European researchers insisted that pyramid shaped containers had strange effects on various objects, changing their biological qualities. These claims are still not proven to the satisfaction of some scientists, yet commercial application of pyramid shaped devices has occurred, indicating that perhaps they do affect the Earth's subtle life-forces.[45]

An indication that this may well be the reason is the discovery made in a secret cavity inside a wall of the Queen's Chamber. This cavity was discovered in the 19th century, and was found to be filled with a very fine sand. Yet it is sand that has been brought in from a far away location, not from the easily available sand lying all around the plateau Giza itself! Just what the difference is between this sand and that of the sand at Giza, remains unknown. But it is clear that only a special kind of sand would suffice, perhaps one which had the appropriate Ch'i quality. This is one more indicator that the ancient architects who guided the construction of the Great Pyramid were working with a precise plan, although we don't know what the purpose of some of its features are.

That such a complex and sophisticated monument was intended simply to be a burial place, now appears ever less likely. Especially when we recall that the sarcophagus never had a lid, and the three portcullis rock slabs were never installed. This means that we can consider again the causeways which link all three of the prominent Giza pyramids to the Nile, indirectly, by giving access to specially built water-ways that came off the Nile, a little further away. These causeways are replicated in later pyramids, such as those at Abu Sir, which are certainly burial sites. But we believe that such causeways would also be needed at pyramids used for general religious purposes.

---

[45] Indications of the genuine nature of these claims are only anecdotal; e.g., an organic winegrower in Canada (Summerhill-Vineyard) stores his wine in a 10m high pyramid because customers, unaware of the storage in a pyramid, report that it has a better quality. Many more such examples exist, especially in eastern Europe.

And it is especially likely that the pyramid of Khufu, and that of Khafre at Giza were used extensively for such purposes, indeed for the most solemn and sacred of such religious activity; the spiritual rites upon which the priesthood depended. Whether in pre-literate shamanistic cultures, or in sophisticated religious systems such as those of ancient Egypt, the process of initiation whereby acolytes were taken up through the ranks of sacerdotal life, by becoming ever more attuned to their deity, was enormously important. So a causeway would be needed for funeral ceremonies for those who were to be buried in the vicinity of the pyramid, including nobles and royalty.

But it would also be needed for the sacred spiritual rites, with boats moving along the Nile, through the man-made water-ways which terminated at a causeway. Then, with the boats moored at a causeway, there would be processions of priests and acolytes and other functionaries up to the pyramids or temples. These religious rites were the life-blood of the priesthood, and hence of the entire land, as the priesthood had a central role in the governance of Egypt.

And finally, some thoughts about those shafts. Remember, since the shafts bend on their way up it would be impossible for starlight to shine down for any acolyte who may have been in some kind of initiation ceremony. So any such alignment to stars seems irrelevant, if we view these shafts as a physical conduit of some sort, a conduit which has to point to exactly the right spot in the night sky. And we know that indeed there is no alignment of these shafts, to any set group of stars.

But perhaps these shafts were designed to assist the acolyte in a psychic vision, who was undergoing some kind of initiation process, to be able to experience the energies of the cosmos, of diverse stars. This could also include our sun or even the great distant sun Sirius; because in a partial way they do lead up towards the outside, up to the stars, shining so intensely above the clear desert night. The goal of the acolyte in this sacred site, in any such spiritual experiences, was to achieve union with the sun god, the central being of the solar system, and also to experience the stars and planets, on a spiritual level. So the shafts could have served this aspect of the mystical worldview of the priesthood.

Conclusions:

Astronomical time markers: zodiac Ages?

Designed to serve several purposes, the Great Pyramid was built to last several thousand years; to survive everything including the severe earthquakes to which Egypt is sometimes subject. So the reasons for its construction must be long term. We have seen that the shafts have no alignment to certain stars at all, whether on the meridian or anywhere else.[46] The idea that the pyramid can be dated by this is simply wrong, and the idea that there is an alignment obviously has to be abandoned.

It is quite possible that the Great Pyramid was also designed for other purposes, in addition to being an initiatory-cultic centre, such as the storage of vital historical records of very ancient times. For, according to Manetho (3rd cent BC), a high priest from the very ancient Egyptian town of Heliopolis, the Egyptian priesthood kept records about the pre-history of Egypt going back 36,000 years, and regarded the task of preserving these as very important. This immense monument may also be a repository of ancient artefacts and historical records, carefully placed for posterity in undiscovered chambers, on the eastern side of the Great Pyramid. This is the so-called Chamber of Records. Such additional functions don't need any of these short-term cosmic alignments.

Experts in early Egyptian history have noted that Egyptian civilisation suddenly appeared as a mature culture, perhaps as

---

[46] The meridian is the invisible line in the heavens where stars reach their highest level, before starting to sink back down towards the horizon.

little as one century before the Great Pyramid was built, [47] without any evidence of transition from a primitive hunter-gatherer stage. Egyptian civilisation suddenly rose to a sophisticated level, producing great architectural monuments and other features of civilisation. So, instead of asking, is the time of the construction of the Great Pyramid connected with the priests' concern about any brief alignment of a star, (via a bent or dead-end shaft!), it is better to ask, **was there, in the view of the priests, a time, a special moment, when the pyramid needed to be built**? A time when the gods were calling for its construction, so to speak. A time specified by the needs or dictates of their gods?

The creation of such a magnificent monument, designed to serve multiple purposes, would greatly assist in bringing into full blossom the recent emergence of Egyptian civilisation. It is our conclusion that the Great Pyramid, like other sacred sites, was constructed and dedicated to its special purposes when, according to the mystical insights of the priests, the right moment dawned for the cultural progress of Egypt. What special moment could this have been? This is unknown, but perhaps linked to astronomical-astrological cycles.

But most of the world's older cultures regarded time as moving in cycles, or demarcated by some celestial factor, such as seasonal settings and risings of prominent stars. It is possible, but not definite, that the passage of the sun through the zodiac also played a role here. Hence in these systems, the priests considered that at key moments in the heavens, a new cycle of activity happens on the Earth, bringing with it a special focus to do with the star-beings of their religion or other celestial spiritual factors. It is only in our modern era that time is seen as proceeding in a simple lineal fashion, from point A to point B. The question is, what might have been the right moment in the view of the Egyptian priests, to commence such a massive project as the building of the great pyramid?

---

[47] The age of this great monument is being pushed back by some academics to about 2,750 BC.

117

It is not known what system of celestial marking time was used, if any, in the Old Kingdom. No specific information has come down to us about their possible use of the zodiac as a basis for marking the progress of time. But the timing of the construction of these great monuments may have been linked to a system of marking time created by the motion of the sun through the zodiac. We can simply note that the timing of the construction of the great pyramid is much more likely to coincide with celestial events and cycles, than by short-term pointless alignments of blocked shafts. It is clear that the Great Pyramid was not built when certain stars reached the meridian, as supposedly seen through the bent or sealed shafts (!).

But it is possible that, in the view of the priesthoods, when some mysterious cosmic clock struck the hour and the time was at hand for a new impetus in culture, the priesthood at Heliopolis responded. As we shall see later, this is a reasonable theory, because across a wide swath of the world similar sacred building projects were undertaken at the same time.

The spiritual meaning in the architecture of the Great Pyramid

Lets now see the implications of the research presented in this book. When we looked at the interior of the Great Pyramid, we mentioned the tunnel known as the Descending Passage, and noted that it deviates from being perfectly straight, from one end to the other, by less than ¼ inch (6mm) in the sides, and only 3/10 inch (.75cm) in the ceiling. Now looking again at the diagram of the internal structure of the Great Pyramid, the orthodox view is that this tunnel goes down to what was meant to be the burial chamber of Khufu, but the builders decided that it would not be good enough, so they abandoned it, and build another one a bit higher up.

But a clear logical assessment indicates this orthodox view is flawed. The tunnel was going to be the passageway for the royal funeral entourage with the great coffin, all the furniture for the Pharaoh's after-life, the great statues and other items.

118

So, the passage would have to be enlarged; at its current narrow dimensions, it was only preliminary – so why would the builders, doing their preliminary foray into the subterranean depths, construct a 350 ft tunnel with an accuracy so superb, so bordering on the impossible, as to be almost eerie? In other words, it is clear that the Descending Passageway was a finished, completed passage. It is an astonishing marvel of the master builder's art. So why does it exist?

Already in the nineteenth century, scientists noted that the Descending Passageway, which leads down to the subterranean chamber at the base of the pyramid, could allow a star at its highest point above the horizon, to be seen by someone deep in the passageway. We have seen earlier that this passageway is an integral part of the sacred landscape symbolism of the pyramid. That is, this shaft took the person down into the Netherworld of the serpent Apep, the malignant realm of evil.

In the course of a spiritual rite, the accuracy of the Descending Passage enabled someone who was down in the dismal Well area to see the stars, at a specified time; so long as the swivel door was left open. Seeing this light in the darkness will be the reason for the extraordinary accuracy of its engineering. It is a complete red herring to follow the idea that the alignment of this passageway to a star allows the great pyramid itself to be dated. The only significant star alignment which was visible from the well, occurred about 1,500 after it was constructed.

But it also may have been used to enable the acolyte to experience what medieval mystics called the Dark Night of the Soul. This is an encounter with the potential for un-spiritual tendencies still lurking in the acolyte's soul. At a crucial moment the acolyte could be directed to look up through the Descending Passage and behold a star far above in the dark night sky; no doubt a star significant in the worldview of the Egyptians.

To understand why the Great Pyramid has its unusual internal chambers and corridors, one needs to understand the path to spirituality. If one enters into the path, and finds oneself in the Descending Passage and does not have the right inner compass so to speak, then one goes off in the quest unprepared. The path will take you down into a dark dead-end; namely the Subterranean Chamber. And any little passageway which you find leading off from that pit, will go nowhere. And, since the journey after death is the same journey as the acolyte experiences during initiation, then these lower internal spaces of the monument also symbolize the worst, the darkest, part of the Nether-world. The Egyptian Book of the Dead is quite specific about this dark part of the journey.

But if when proceeding along the Descending Passage of the pyramid, you manage to see the entrance to the Ascending Passage, and start the journey upwards, then things will go much better for you. Eventually you will arrive the Parting of the Ways, and though it is somewhat difficult to see the true entrance, this is where the large corbelled Grand Gallery begins, see illustration 6. You also have to avoid a cavity in the floor which takes one down the perilous Well Shaft into the subterranean chamber.

So you could end up down there (again); and this is a reminder that spiritual regression is still possible; see illustration 6. You will probably find the entrance to the tunnel straight ahead that takes you to the Queen's Chamber, although it is obscured by a stone. In that case, you avoid the passage downwards, and find yourself eventually in a better place, the Queen's Chamber. And in fact the possibility exists that in this Chamber the acolyte was offered some form of initial spiritual experience.

But, furthermore, if the acolyte had sufficient alertness and courage as he entered the Grand Gallery, he could look upwards, as he exited the Ascending Passage, not just down or straight ahead. Anyone looking up at this point would discern a low wall rising abruptly upwards, a couple of metres above his head, dimly evident in the light of the oil torch. It is the beginning of another, much better pathway. This is the elevated walkway through the Grand Gallery. With effort, getting a toehold into the niches carved in the vertical walls, one could clamber one's way up and onto this walkway, and walk through the Grand Gallery, which proceeds along for 157 ft, and has a height of 28 ft (48m x 8.5m).

Now, we noted earlier that the Grand Gallery is a strangely shaped large corridor, which leads on to the initiatory chamber. The purpose of this design becomes clear when the spiritual purpose of the Great Pyramid is perceived. It is corbelled, that is, as we noted earlier, it tapers inwards at the top, in seven stages, see illustration 13.

The Grand Gallery is in effect a long, narrow corridor, some 61 inches wide at the bottom, but narrowing down to 41 inches at the top (1.6m to 1m). This design is intended to remind the acolyte that they are seeking access to the seven realms of the spirit. And remember, precisely the same reminder is part of the after-life teachings of the Egyptian religion. It is a difficult arduous climb, even more so in ancient times, without the benefit of modern handrails and wooden steps.

The pitch torch of an acolyte would illumine the receding, narrowing space, creating a potent metaphor for the journey up to the ever more sublime higher spirit realms, arching above them, which they were seeking. As they make their way up, they manoeuvre around the three stone slabs that many centuries later shall be slid down into the Ascending Passage to stop any accessing the chambers. These three slabs of dense matter blocking the path, may have symbolized the hindrances posed by the feelings, the intelligence and the intentions in so far as they have taken on earthly qualities.

But also as the acolyte slowly ascends, they notice 28 rectangular holes cut into the passageway at regular intervals, on the sides of the walkway, see illustration 13. These 28 cavities would have encouraged them to contemplate the activity of their revered god, Osiris, the same deity whom they

13

Inside the Grand Gallery

Looking towards the King's Chamber.

In this photo, the seven-tiered narrowing of the chamber can be clearly seen.

were hoping to encounter in the three day process inside the King's Chamber. Osiris is a solar god, but he also has a relationship to the Moon's energies; as after all these two celestial bodies are themselves interlinked. Osiris, when viewed as a lunar deity, was called Osiris-Aah and is depicted with the crescent moon above his head, inside of which is the sun disc. Consequently, it is not surprising that Plutarch reports that Osiris ruled (or lived) for 28 years; and comments that this feature of his nature refers actually to the 28 day lunar cycle.[48] (30)

Once in the King's Chamber the acolyte would undergo some mysterious initiatory experience in that granite sarcophagus, underneath a five-tiered granite ceiling, a design which perhaps enhanced some unknown subtle energy. This is a more likely reason for the strange internal structure of the Great Pyramid, than a tomb. When we read religious-spiritual architecture from an ancient holistic culture in an holistic way, we can discern the underlying motive of the building, and the spiritual message which it embodies.

It seems evident that the Great Pyramid was a monument designed to be used as part of the general religious activity of the 4th Dynasty priesthood, in particular for the spiritual rites of the priesthood. And it was also no doubt hoped that it would be so used for many centuries; and it was possibly linked by underground tunnels to the sphinx. Very importantly, all this does not exclude the role of the pyramid in a funeral ritual for Khufu; and this is where the mainstream Egyptologists can find resolution to the conflict between their view of it as a tomb, and the alternative insightful view, of seeing its initiatory features.

Khufu no doubt arranged for the Great Pyramid to be involved in his funeral and after-life rituals. That is, his mummy would have been taken up the ramp from the waterway, to his Valley Temple where certain aspects of the after-life ritual were

---

[48] The moon has 5 cycles around us, 4 of these are completed every 28 days.

performed. And then from there a procession went up the long causeway to the ritual temple (or mortuary temple) by the eastern side of the Great Pyramid.

Many processions would have taken this same route over many centuries, for religious purposes; that is, to carry out initiatory rites inside the Great Pyramid. Further rites would be performed near the Great Pyramid, and then his mummy was entombed in a secret place, not in the known chambers of the pyramid. It was placed either in a secret chamber inside the pyramid, or perhaps somewhere underneath the vast monument. And for a millennium or two thereafter, acolytes would enter the concealed swivel door up on the north wall, and begin their perilous journey through the tunnels in their quest for union with the divine.

Appendix

The key points about the Sphinx

Has discarded tools etc deep inside it, originating from the Old Kingdom era

Carved approximately in the time of pharaoh Khafre, ca. 2,700 BC

Is weathered by moisture-soaked sand covering its body for millennia, activating a salt corrosion process

Represents an aspect of the sun-god called Harmakhis

Is shaped partly as a lion, because lions were viewed as solar beings, and the sun's energies are maximal when in Leo, as Sirius brings the Nile's life-renewing floods

The key points about the Great Pyramid

Has the genuine cartouche of Pharaoh Khufu inside it

Was constructed ca. 2,800 – 2,600 BC

Represents the primeval Earth's Ben-Ben shape

Is pyramidal-shaped in reference to Earth's tectonic properties

Has engineering features which are beyond 19th century technology

Incorporates an architectural sacred landscape

Its mirrored-walls announced when the equinox was approaching

Was used for spiritual-religious purpose, not only as a tomb

Its internal chambers are patterned on initiation wisdom of Hermes

Perhaps not all of its internal chambers have been discovered

May have an undiscovered chamber for ancient documents/artefacts

May reflect the pattern of Orion's belt

Hidden tunnels and chambers

Despite being such a central sacred site to the old Egyptian priesthoods, and the Great Pyramid being an initiatory building, so far no tunnels have been found which connect the sphinx to the Great Pyramid. It has long been believed that a tunnel links the sphinx to the Great Pyramid and this may still be the case; however no reliable evidence of such a tunnel system has as yet been found. In 2006 Egyptian archaeologists undertook detailed investigations, under the direction of Dr. Mohammad Abbas, using GPR (ground penetrating radar) of the area around the two largest pyramids.

They found a number of significant things; two shafts were located near the southern side of Khufu's pyramid, the other near the Khafre Causeway. And also two subterranean chambers, or possibly naturally occurring cavities, were found, one near to the entrance door to the Sphinx (on the north side), and one on the eastern side Khafre's pyramid. To date, there has been no news of any discoveries being made in regard to these places.

There are actually quite a number of claims of either tunnels or secret underground chambers having been discovered. But no real evidence has ever been produced to back up such claims, and often hearsay or convenient assumptions are used to make the claim more convincing or sensational. But we saw how the references to the great sphinx strongly indicated that it was carved during the Old Kingdom, and that the Cairo area was really important to the Egyptian mystical worldview.

This affirms the conclusion that the Great Pyramid was constructed about 2,800-2,600 BC on the Giza plateau, because it was during the Old Kingdom that this area was regarded as a representation of the Creation of the world, and was made the site of major events in Egyptian mythology. On the plateau there is a unique complex of pyramids, tunnels, temples, mortuary chambers, and statues (both below and above ground), all of which are to do with either life after-death or the quest for spiritual consciousness.

The technical difficulties of building the Great Pyramid
The conclusion also appears accurate that the Great Pyramid is a monument whose construction was made possible not only

by sheer muscle work and clever construction techniques, but also possibly by some form of mental faculty, unknown to us today. It also appears likely that the priests were able to induce a state of mind in the workers, which enhanced their capacity to achieve such extremely difficult construction work, rather like the chanting used in some earlier societies, who knew that a rhythmical pattern of work made the effort easier. It also appears possible that some kind of technology, unknown to us today, was used to augment muscle power and ramps or pulleys. The total weight of the stone slabs used in the building of the Great Pyramid is estimated to be about six million tonnes.

The question of just how such a vast monument was actually constructed is still unresolved, although the current view amongst Egyptologists is that one or more ramps were used to build the huge monument. It is very likely that some form of ramp was used, and also that muscle-power was important; ancient Egyptian drawings show men hauling statues along on flat-bottomed sledges, etc. But many people quite reasonably don't accept that the use of ramps alone could have made it possible. Ramps of a limited size may well have been part of the procedure used, but ramps and sheer manpower do not explain all the achievements involved.

Mathematicians and engineers (such as the Danish expert Garde-Hanson, and the Egyptian professor, Assam Deif) have pointed out that an external ramp is unlikely to be the full solution. For the ramp would itself be much larger than the entire mass of the Great Pyramid, and its construction alone would involve an earth-moving project on a scale beyond the capacity of nearly any nation at any time.

(Think of the difficulty in bringing two vast mountainous masses of soil to the plateau, since there is not much to be found on the plateau.) Certainly large numbers of Egyptian peasants were called upon to spend months each year working at the construction task, and their muscle power was important here, but some other factor must have been at work as well.

For an intriguing version of the mainstream view of how they were built, see engineer Franz Löhner's website, the text is in English and German, and it has excellent diagrams.[49]

Löhner also has concluded that external ramps are just not feasible, "It was not necessary, and is not technically possible to build ramps to do this, because they would be hundreds of thousands of cubic metres in size, and more than 100 metres high." He offers an alternative clever engineering solution to the problem. We need to bear in mind that the pyramid of Khafre is nearly as massive as Khufu's, so two virtually mountain-size monuments of stone had to be constructed, so two vast mountains of soil would have to be obtained, formed into ramps – if ramps were used – and then disposed of.

Just as there are still clear signs of the rock quarries and hollows from which the millions and millions of tons of rock were taken for the pyramids, one would think that there would still be, even today, some signs of the vast soil-quarry (totalling approximately three times the combined mass of both pyramids, or about 30 million tons) from which the soil was taken for these two massive projects.

To put this into perspective, there is enough stone in the Great Pyramid to build thirty Empire State buildings, or in the famous conclusion of Napoleon, enough to build a wall 3 metres high (9.84 ft) and 30cm (11.81 in) thick around the entire boundary of France. One has to nearly double this, to include the huge pyramid of Khafre!

Traditionalists who support this theory of manpower and simple pulleys and sledges, unassisted by some other unknown force, will refer to the successful building of a tiny pyramid, only some 18ft high (5.5m), using pulleys and teams of men. But this is not a real test, for the vast proportions of the Great Pyramid mean much greater heights and much larger stone slabs would have to be manoeuvred, and that is only the

---

[49] www.cheops-pyramide.ch/Khufu-pyramid

beginning of the difficulties. As we have seen, extraordinary alignments have to be achieved as well. Although as Dr. Hawass's team has found evidence of some kind of ramps, it appears that small ramps were also involved in some way.

In fact, in 1978 a team from Japan were given permission to try to build a duplicate pyramid near the Great Pyramid, some 60 ft high, to test the mainstream theory of its construction; i.e., that muscle power and purely primitive methods were used. The team was totally unable, using just one-ton blocks of stone, to build their 60ft pyramid. They could not even float them across the Nile, let alone move them across the sand; nor could they hoist them up, even with the help of ramps.

Some Works Consulted

The Works of the Emperor Julian, trans. Wilmer C. Wright, W. Heinemann, New York, 1953

S.H. Ford, The Great Pyramid of Egypt, Health Research, California, 1973

J. Baines & J. Malek, Atlas of Ancient Egypt, Equinox Books, Oxford, 1991

J. G. Wilkinson, The ancient Egyptians, Studio Editions, London, 1988

J.C. Cooper, An Illustrated Encyclopaedia of Traditional Symbols, Thames & Hudson, London, 1978

Peter Tompkin's book, Secrets of the Great Pyramid, now somewhat dated, and not discriminating between rumour and fact, provides an overview of the history of research undertaken into the great pyramid, and of the various theories about its purpose and construction.

E. Cayce, The Egyptian Heritage, ARE Press, Virginia, 1974

E. Cayce, My Life as a Seer, edit. A.R, Smith, St. Martin's press, New York 1997

A. Collins, Gods of Eden, Headline, London, 1998

S.H. Ford, The Great Pyramid of Egypt, Health Research, California, 1973

Alan Gardiner, The Egyptians, The Folio Soc., London, 1961

Griffith F. & Thompson, H., The Leyden Papyrus, Dover Press, N.Y. 1974

P. Lemesurier, The Great Pyramid decoded, Element Books, Wiltshire, 1977

J. Ray, Reflections of Osiris, Profile Books, London, 2001

J. Romer, Ancient Lives, Guild Publishing, London, 1984

I. Schaller de Lubicz, Her-Bak, Egyptian Initiate, Inner Traditions, no date

Rudolf Steiner, Christianity as Mystical Fact; Egyptian Myths.

R. Temple, The Sirius Mystery, Destiny Books, no date

Tiradritti, F., The Cairo Museum Masterpieces of Egyptian Art, T & H, London 1998

M. Toth, Pyramid Prophecies, Destiny Books, Rochester, 1988

E. A. Wallis-Budge, The Gods of the Egyptians, 2 Vols, Dover Press, New York, 1969
E. A. Wallis-Budge, Osiris, the Egyptian religion of Resurrection, Univ. Bks, N.Y. 1961
E. A. Wallis-Budge, The Egyptian Heaven and Hell, Open Court, Illinois, 1989
E. A. Wallis-Budge, Egyptian Magic, Dover Press, N.Y. 1971

Illustration Credits

1 The author
2 The author
3 The author
4 The author
5 The author
6 The author
7 With kind permission of Ruth Shilling of All One World Tours; see her "Beloved Egypt" website; www.belovedegypt.com/34
(The use by myself of this graphic does not imply that the owner of it in any way shares or agrees with my perspective on this subject.)
8 Privately owned.
9 The author
10 Privately owned.
11 The author
12 From the excellent website of Frank Doernenburg, www. doernenburg.alien.de/alternativ.
(The use by myself of this graphic does not imply that the owner of it in any way shares or agrees with my perspective on this subject.)
13 Privately owned.

INDEX

www.ingramcontent.com/pod-product-compliance
Lightning Source LLC
Chambersburg PA
CBHW081330090426
42737CB00017B/3085